Lecture Notes in Computer Science　　8277

Commenced Publication in 1973
Founding and Former Series Editors:
Gerhard Goos, Juris Hartmanis, and Jan van Leeuwen

Christopher Nugent   Antonio Coronato
José Bravo (Eds.)

Ambient Assisted Living and Active Aging

5th International Work-Conference, IWAAL 2013
Carrillo, Costa Rica, December 2-6, 2013
Proceedings

 Springer

Volume Editors

Christopher Nugent
University of Ulster
Faculty of Computing and Engineering
School of Computing and Mathematics
Newtownabbey BT37 0QB, County Antrim, UK
E-mail: cd.nugent@ulster.ac.uk

Antonio Coronato
ICAR-CNR
80131 Napoli, Italy
E-mail: coronato.a@na.icar.cnr.it

José Bravo
MAmI Research Lab
Castilla-La Manca University
13071 Ciudad Real, Spain
E-mail: jose.bravo@uclm.es

ISSN 0302-9743   e-ISSN 1611-3349
ISBN 978-3-319-03091-3   e-ISBN 978-3-319-03092-0
DOI 10.1007/978-3-319-03092-0
Springer Cham Heidelberg New York Dordrecht London

CR Subject Classification (1998): H.5.2-3, J.3-4, C.2, H.4, H.3, K.4.2, D.2

LNCS Sublibrary: SL 3 – Information Systems and Application, incl. Internet/Web
and HCI

Typesetting: Camera-ready by author, data conversion by Scientific Publishing Services, Chennai, India

Printed on acid-free paper

Springer is part of Springer Science+Business Media (www.springer.com)

Preface

This volume contains the work presented at the 5th International Work Conference on Ambient Assisted Living (IWAAL 2013) held in Costa Rica during the 2nd–6th December, 2013. The event was established during 2009, inspired by the European Union's Ambient Assisted Living Joint Program (AALJP). The ageing of the population is concerning national healthcare systems throughout all developed countries in relation to the increasing burdens being placed on the provision of health and social care. Predictions are estimating that by 2020 around one quarter of the European population will be over 65. This will make healthcare systems almost unable to sustain an adequate delivery of care provision unless new models of care and prevention are introduced. The AALJP has as a core strategy to support the development of solutions to improve the delivery of care and increase levels of independence for an ageing population.

Information and Communication Technologies are paving the way towards a new paradigm of advanced systems aimed at both preventing and managing long term healthcare conditions in addition to de-hospitalizing care provision. The interest of healthcare stakeholders is continuously growing around such technological based solutions which aim to address the effects of the ageing of the population. As a result, Ambient Assisted Living (AAL) is becoming a well recognized domain. AAL relates to the use of ICT technologies and services in both daily living and working environments with the aim to help inhabitants by preventing and improving wellness and health conditions, in addition to assisting with daily activities, promotion of staying active, remaining socially connected, and of living independently.

The theme of this year's event is *Ambient Assisted Living and Active Aging*. This year, once again, IWAAL collected a remarkable set of scientific works reporting new methods, methodologies, algorithms, and tools specifically devised to address AAL research challenges. In addition, a variety of assistive applications that harness the benefits of sensing technologies, human computer interaction, and ambient intelligence have been included.

The review process of the material submitted was supported by over 60 members from an International Program Committee. This included members from the following countries in Europe: Czech Republic, Northern Ireland, Spain, Italy, Austria, Belgium, England, Germany, The Netherlands, France and Cyprus and was further supported by members from the United States of America, Canada, Mexico, Chile, Panama and Costa Rica. Each paper was allocated up to 3 reviewers with the final process of the review being guided by the two workshop co-chairs.

From the 23 papers submitted, 13 were accepted as full papers and 7 were recommended to revise and re-submit their original submissions as short papers. The final set of papers represents a truly international field of research with authors from 12 countries including: Jordan, Mexico, Costa Rica, Chile, United States of America, South Korea, Austria, England, Spain, Sweden, Finland and Northern Ireland.

To conclude, we wish to thank all organizers, members of the Program Committee and reviewers for helping us in realizing a top quality conference and producing this volume.

December 2013

Christopher Nugent
Antonio Coronato
José Bravo

Organization

General Chairs

José Bravo   Castilla La Mancha University, Spain
Sergio F. Ochoa   University of Chile, Chile

IWAAL PC Chairs

Christopher Nugent   University of Ulster, UK
Antonio Coronato   CNR, Italy

Workshop Chair

Ramón Hervás   Castilla La Mancha University, Spain

Local Chair

Luis A. Guerrero   Universidad de Costa Rica, Costa Rica

Publicity Chairs

Jesus Fontecha   Castilla La Mancha University, Spain
Vladimir Villarreal   Technological University of Panama, Panama

Program Committee

Julio Abascal   University of the Basque Country-Euskal Herriko Unibertsitatea, Spain
Bessan Abdulrazak   Université de Sherbrooke, Canada
Xavier Alamán   UAM, Spain
Rosa Arriaga   Georgia Institute of Technology, USA
Mohamed Bakhouya   University of Technology at Belfort Montbeliard, France
Stephane Bouchard   Université du Québec en Outaouais, Canada
Kyle Boyd   University of Ulster, UK
Robin Braun   University of Technology Sydney, Australia
José Bravo   Castilla La Mancha University, Spain
Yang Cai   Carnegie Mellon University, USA

Luis Carriço	University of Lisbon, Portugal
Liming Luke Chen	University of Ulster, UK
Wei Chen	Eindhoven University of Technology, The Netherlands
Vaclav Chudadek	Czech Technical University of Prague, Czech Republic
Marcello Cinque	The University of Naples Federico II, Italy
Ian Cleland	University of Ulster, UK
Walter Colitti	ETRO-COMO, Vrije Universiteit Brussel, Belgium
Antonio Coronato	ICAR-CNR, Italy
Hariton Costing	University of Medicine and Pharmacy, Romania
Domenico Cotroneo	University of Naples Federico II, Italy
Vicenzo de Florio	University of Antwerp, Belgium
Wolfgang De Meuter	Vrije Universiteit Brussel, Belgium
Giuseppe de Pietro	CNR, Italy
Giovanna Di Marzio	University of Geneva, Switzerland
Jesús Fontecha	Castilla La Mancha University, Spain
Leonardo Galicia	UABC, Mexico
Antonio Garcia-Macias	CICESE, Mexico
Antonietta Grasso	Xerox Research Center Europe, France
Dominique Guinard	MIT/ETH Zurich/SAP Research, Switzerland
Phillip Hartin	University of Ulster, UK
Jan Havlik	Czech Technical University of Prague, Czech Republic
Sumi Helal	University of Florida, USA
Ramon Hervas	Castilla La Mancha University, Spain
Martin Hitz	Alpen Adria Universitat Klagenfurt, Austria
Robert Istepanian	Kingston University, UK
Martin Kampel	Vienna University of Technology, Austria
Wolfgang Kastner	TU Vienna, Austria
Abdelmajid Khelil	Huawei ERC, Germany
Bernhard Klein	Deusto Institute of Technology, Spain
Vaclav Kremen	Czech Technical University of Prague, Czech Republic
Lenka Lhotska	Czech Technical University of Prague, Czech Republic
Vincenzo Loia	Università degli Studi di Salerno, Italy
Wolfram Luther	University of Duisburg-Essen, Germany
Diego López-De-Ipiña	University of Deusto, Spain
Pedro Jose Marron	University of Duisburg-Essen and Fraunhofer IAIS, Germany
Oscar Mayora	Create-Net, Italy
Vittorio Miori	CNR, Italy

Angelica Munoz-Melendez INAOE, Mexico
Tasuya Nakayima
Panagiota Nikopoulou-Smyrni Brunel University, UK
Christopher Nugent University of Ulster, UK
Sergio Ochoa Universidad de Chile, Chile
Cristiano Paggetti I+ S.r.l, Italy
George Papadopoulos University of Cyprus, Cyprus
Dennis Pfisterer University of Lübeck, Germany
Till Plumbaum DAI-Labor, Technische Universität Berlin,
 Germany
Josef Rafferty University of Ulster, UK
Marcela Rodriguez UABC, Mexico
Mario Romero Georgia Institute of Technology, USA
Rodrigo Santos Universidad Nacional del Sur - Bahía Blanca,
 Argentina
Monica Tentori CICESE, Mexico
Gabriel Urzaiz University of Anáhuac Mayab, Mexico
Natalia Villanueva University of Texas at El Paso, USA
Vladimir Villarreal Technological University of Panama, Panama
Andreas Voss University of Applied Sciences Jena, Germany
Nadir Weibel University of California San Diego, USA
Hen-I Yang Iowa State University, USA

Additional Reviewers

Borja Gamecho University of the Basque Country, Spain
Christos Mettouris University of Cyprus, Cyprus
Peter Rothenpieler University of Lubeck, Germany
Eline Philips Vrije Universiteit Brussel, Belgium

Table of Contents

Session 3: Sensing and Activity Recognition

Session 4: Key Application Domains

A Knowledge Based Framework to Support Active Aging at Home Based Environments

Miguel Ángel Valero[1], José Bravo[2], Juan Manuel García[3],
Diego López-de-Ipiña[4], and Ana Gómez[1]

[1] Dep. of Telematic Enginering and Architectures, Universidad Politécnica de Madrid, Spain
{mavalero,agomez}@diatel.upm.es
[2] MAmI Research Lab, Universidad de Castilla La Mancha, Ciudad Real, Spain
Jose.Bravo@uclm.es
[3] Universidad de Alicante, Spain
juanma@dtic.ua.es
[4] MORE Lab, Universidad de Deusto, Bilbao, Spain
dipina@eside.deusto.es

Abstract. Information and Communication Technologies can support Active Aging strategies in a scenario like the Smart Home. This paper details a person centered distributed framework, called TALISMAN+, whose aim is to promote personal autonomy by taking advantage of knowledge based technologies, sensors networks, mobile devices and internet. The proposed solution can support an elderly person to keep living alone at his house without being obliged to move to a residential center. The framework is composed by five subsystems: a reasoning module that is able to take local decisions at home in order to support active aging, a biomedical variables telemonitorisation platform running on a mobile device, a hybrid reasoning middleware aimed to assess cardiovascular risk in a remote way, a private vision based sensor subsystem, and a secure telematics solution that guarantees confidentiality for personal information. TALISMAN+ framework deployment is being evaluated at a real environment like the Accessible Digital Home.

Keywords: Active aging, smart home, collaborative reasoning agents, sensors.

1   Framework Contextualization

Active Aging is not just a set of recommendations for physical and psychological well-being but a "process of optimizing opportunities for health, participation and security in order to enhance quality of life as people age" [1]. The World Health Organization (WHO) highlights the necessity to promote effective strategies and solutions that maintain autonomy as a person grows older. Many daily life activities are carried out at the home environment and this user domain is widely surrounded by multiple devices and appliances which are supposed to make our life "easier".

The interoperation at home of these available mechanic, electronic, information and communication technologies, sets the basis to provide the elderly population

C. Nugent, A. Coronato, and J. Bravo (Eds.): IWAAL 2013, LNCS 8277, pp. 1–8, 2013.
© Springer International Publishing Switzerland 2013

and/or people with neurodegenerative diseases with accessible services to promote personal autonomy. Cheek et al. mention the concept of aging-in-place and point out different facilities to be supported by Smart Home (SH) technologies such as "emergency care, fall prevention & detection, reminder systems and assistance for those with cognitive impairments" [2]. This idea is not new, some authors like Williams et al. described in 1998 their future smart home for "the provision of artificial intelligence -AI- based information processing and the management of decision-making structures required" [3]. Fifteen years later, users could request for SH technologies at their house since environmental sensors like presence, motion, fire, flood or gas are market available; biomedical data devices can be connected to measure pulse, temperature, glucose or blood pressure, and reasoning middleware environments are highly usable. However, the easy to use and knowledge based person centered interaction with these devices is still not solved especially to support aforementioned SH facilities. TALISMAN+, the distributed framework detailed in this research paper, aims to go one step forward in this direction by offering an integrated solution that encompasses local and remote reasoning modules, biomedical mobile connected telemonitoring devices, environmental sensor networks and security mechanisms that guarantee privacy and confidentiality of supported homecare telematic services. The framework core has been designed and developed by taking into account the necessities of two users domains: vulnerable people with Parkinson disease and persons with mobility restrictions.

Information and communication technologies can help people with cognitive and mobility impairments to promote Active Aging activities related to communication, stimulation and environmental control. Laiseca et al. showed the utilization of these technologies to assist the elderlies with cognitive disabilities by using memory games that facilitate information to caregivers and relatives [4]. Activity recognition can be triggered both from data driven information provided by users or through the utilization of sensor-based recognition. Chen et al. compare these two approaches and conclude that Knowledge-Driven models need to handle uncertainty and time in order to distinguish intent or goal recognition [5]. Ontology-based systems have been tested to support active health with mobile technologies. Docksteader et al. published a Mobile Ontology-based Reasoning and Feedback system that monitors SpO2, using Semantic Web Rule Language (SWRL) and communicate them via SMS and HTTP protocols [6]. Health care domain has also experimented with the use of cameras in private spaces in the field of Ambient-Assisted Living (AAL) and aging in place. Cardinaux et al. reviewed in 2011 the pros and contras, related to user´s acceptance, reliable reasoning and privacy, of video based technology for AAL [7].

No doubt that TALISMAN+ framework provides facilities that can be critical for the security of the elderly. Therefore, privacy of monitored individuals should be guaranteed at the same time its identities are checked as Islam et al. states for SH [8]. Since sensors and devices used can be perceived as an intrusive element at home [12], privacy and authentication issues were considered an essential part of this framework in order to reinforce the trust of users to promote their personal autonomy.

2   User Driven Design Methodology

Further to ANSI/IEEE 1471-2000 conceptual framework for architecture description, TALISMAN+ design can be decomposed in five architectural views. The methods provided by this standard helped to describe the global view of the solution according to a user driven approach. Thus, people with cognitive or mobility restrictions, such as the elderly, become the main stakeholder addressed by each of the five deployed subsystems. The mission is to support autonomous active aging at home by providing context-aware reactions triggered by detected events, user profiles and reasoning procedures. Main concerns addressed in this framework deal with security, accessibility, reliable reasoning and interoperability. Security view followed a user centered approach so that an aging person may feel trust about his or her interaction with the system. Therefore, user requirements analysis led to define a user interface so that all the stakeholders may simulate, check and effectively validate the suggestions provided by the framework. These stakeholders include the elderly person, informal caregivers, relatives, and professionals in charge such us geriatricians, therapists, social workers or nurses.

By following a user driven design methodology, replicable user cases were defined according to the knowledge acquired from two users´ entities: Madrid Parkinson´s disease association and the association of people with spinal injury and physical disabilities (ASPAYM). As Gass et al. state for internet-based services, the specification of end-user-driven data acquirement at the SH was a critical issue to define context-aware interoperable facilities to promote active aging [9].

Fig. 1 details the functional Framework design whose user driven main use case is detailed as follow: 1) Biomedical data provided by users through mobile connected sensors is sent to the reasoning subsystems; 2) the hybrid remote reasoner validates a user profile (e.g. level of risk disease) and sends this data to the local reasoner; 3) environmental context and user profile info is updated to the local reasoner; 4) a descriptive local reasoner suggests actions at the SH for active aging; 5) the security view ensures authentication, confidentiality and integrity of managed information.

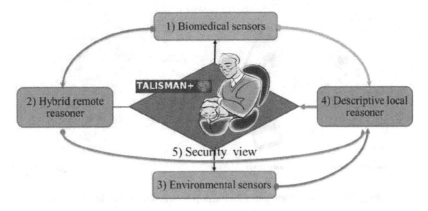

Fig. 1. User-driven functional Framework Design

3   Development Results

The resulting distributed framework is described in the following parts by following the user-driven context previously depicted. :

3.1   Mobile Monitoring (MoMo) Platform

The Mobile Monitoring platform (MoMo) allows aging patients to having continuous diseases control and direct communication with their doctor. MoMo enables patient mobile telemonitoring by using biometric devices (e.g. glucometers, blood pressure meters) to send data to a mobile phone via technologies such as WiFi, NFC or Bluetooth [10]. An ontological architecture has been created in order to catalogue the elements and provide TALISMAN+ local and remote reasoners with ad hoc feedback.

Patient monitoring represents one of the key elements in the progress and control of his illness. This monitoring provides patient and doctor with continuous data about disease´s status (vital signs, pulse glucose) so that, the doctor can accordingly readjust the initial treatments and prescriptions. Mobile phone is the selected technology as it is fairly used by aging people and can support daily activities for communication and information management. A group of ontologies called MoMOntology represent the ontologies of mobile monitoring process and allow to model the data collected from biometrics devices. An analytical engine, described in 3.2 which combines Fuzzy Logic and probabilistic reasoning, allows managing patient records based on an analysis of past situations to predict future difficulties like variations in vital signs). MoMo takes advantage of mobile phones and biometric devices to facilitate patient monitoring as data is recorded in a central server to be used by TALISMAN+ framework.

Fig. 2 shows the developed platform. On the left, healthcare and monitoring devices are connected to Bluetooth mobile devices. In the center, these biometric devices are linked to a mobile phone to process sensor data, manage applications, and ensure redundant connectivity via 3G and WiFi data networks. Information is transmitted to a central database and advisory system for evaluation by the medical server (right).

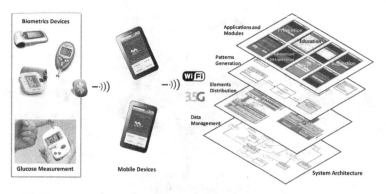

Fig. 2. MoMo platform and relationship between data and device entities

3.2   Hybrid Cooperative Reasoner

As stated in TALISMAN+ framework, a middleware is requested to facilitate context capture from any device, including embedded ones, to program environment's reactivity. TALIS+Engine is the susbsystem were the ontology AMBI2ONT was created to model ambiguity in its two facets, uncertainty and vagueness, together with sensor fusion and reasoning inference engine. Upon uncertainty, the certainty factor (CF) of contextual data is modeled. Vagueness consideration allows model unclearly defined situations like cold room or noise room where different users have different perceptions. Such ontology models places, things in those places such as devices or people, capabilities and linguistic terms. Fig. 3 shows a ContextData individual with a sensor value associated a certainty degree about the credibility of such measure and a set of linguistic terms where each term is associated with a membership function. Thus, in this case the temperature sensor in a given room can be considered mainly hot. Once the measures are modeled considering the uncertainty and the vagueness of the data, semantic inference process is applied, so that implicit data is derived from explicit data. For example, the location associated to each measure is determined, knowing the location of the temperature sensor. Subsequently, a data fusion process is applied which aggregates measures of the same type (e.g. temperature sensor) within the same container (e.g. room). Two different strategies are supported: tourney (the best) and combination, where depending on the scheme applied the best, worst or average measure can be considered. Thus, the temperature values of all sensors within a room are combined.

Finally, the behavior rules defined for an extension of the JFuzzyLogic fuzzy logic engine [13] are executed. Such engine was modified to incorporate to it treatment of both uncertain data and rules. An example of the now supported syntax, which extends JFuzzyLogic engine's Fuzzy control language (FCL), is shown on the bottom left hand side of Fig. 3, where both uncertainty (CF 1) and vagueness (HOT) are considered:

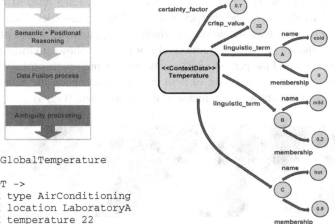

```
RULE CF 1
LaboratoryA hasGlobalTemperature
temperatureX
temperatureX HOT ->
airCoditioningX type AirConditioning
airCoditioningX location LaboratoryA
airCoditioningX temperature 22
```

Fig. 3. Hybrid reasoner uncertainty management and AMBI2ONT Ontology

3.3   Vision Based Sensor Subsystem

TALISMAN+ distributed framework relies on private sensoring solutions at the SH to make ad hoc local reasoning to promote healthy and social activities related to active aging. Vision@home is the integrated subsystem that includes a technological infrastructure and vision-based services to monitor and recognize the activity of users at home, including the privacy protection of who perceived with these vision devices. Thus, a double functionality is achieved: dynamically modeling of habitual behavior of people to detect events that may identify abnormal behaviors, and confidential vision-based services to detect and recognize objects and people of interest in the scene and characterization and interpretation of movement to monitor their activity.

Static cameras, pan-tilt, omni-directional and low cost devices RGB-D, like Kinect, were applied to allow better interpretation of motion without forgetting ethical aspects when monitoring people in private spaces. Two cases were addressed to recognize human activity: action recognition using several cameras and action recognition using Kinects. The implemented system recognizes, through cameras, simple actions such as walking, jumping, running and falling. Anonymous people silhouettes are gathered using background removal and next features invariant to scaling and rotation. During recognition, the position of the person is determined at every moment by matching the sequence of postures with the Knowledge Base using Dynamic Time Warping. The system operates at video rate, which is one of the main requirements. Regarding the recognition of actions using Kinects, a classification system was developed from skeletal actions of a person. Thus, Microsoft SDK and OpenNI library functions were tested and positions recognized by Growing Neural Gas. The optimal set of characteristics that increases the accuracy of action recognition algorithm was founded by using evolutionary learning techniques [11]. Fall detection service and other actions are supported by a simple prototype that determines the fall by calculating the hip height.

A context oriented privacy protection model was defined based on levels. Each level defines the nature of the information that will be provided to TALISMAN+ local reasoner or even shown to an authorized caregiver. Each level of representation can depend on the event and the permissions of the stakeholder. Four protection levels were verified as feasible: no alarm, which displays a virtual image of the environment without showing any person; low level alarm, which shows a virtual image of both the environment and the person, showing its location but not its posture; high level alarm, which shows a virtual image of both the environment and the person; and very high level alarm that shows a real image of the environment (Fig. 4).

Fig. 4. Vision based privacy degrees depending on the level of alarm

3.4   Local Logic Description Reasoner and Security View

The distributed framework proposed provides functionality in a home environment where critical assurance of privacy is needed for the elderly. Local reasoning should confirm individuals' identities and ensure privacy when they are monitored. Very often, sensors and devices used for these services are perceived as an intrusive element at home. Therefore, privacy and authentication was considered an essential part of TALISMAN+ not just to protect communications but to reinforce users' trust in the use of the news services for active aging and promotion of personal autonomy.

Bearing in mind this user-centered approach, the SH logs all interactions of sensors and monitoring systems that are managing data with the database as well as the data exchanged between the SH and telecare centers. In this way, users with cognitive or physical impairments gain access at any time to the information obtained from the logs, as the system enables tangible and understandable interaction when coupling sensors and actuators into actions. These actions allow users to mentally represent the capabilities of the SH where they perform their daily tasks, regardless of the complexity of the underlying ubiquitous system. The framework implemented a security agent in charge of sending, securing and logging the outward interactions. Fig. 5 shows this agent that receives data from SH and establishes a secure SSL channel between home and telecare entities to provide two-way authentication, non-repudiation, confidentiality and integrity services for the exchange. Previous images processing by the vision based sensor subsystem, this agent sends a virtual hidden image of people at home.

For this purpose it was defined an XML register document that contents the complete sequence of interactions that take place between the server and the smart home as a result of the execution of the service. After ensuring the security of communications for the house with the outside, there is still an important point to solve referred to the way that people at home are identified. Mutual authentication in SSL requires users must be in possession of the corresponding X.509 certificate to operate the system.

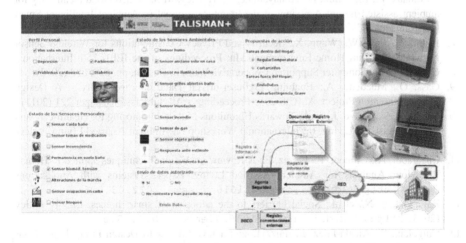

Fig. 5. TALISMAN+ security supporting local reasoning engine

4   Conclusions

The deployment of TALISMAN+ framework at the Accessible Digital Home allows testing a sustainable telecare service with users from Parkinson and Cordial Injury associations. This stage will be initiated shortly once the development and integration stages are completed in order to check reliable reasoning, security and performance.

Acknowledgments. Authors would like to thank the National Plan for Science, Development and Innovation of the Spanish Ministry for Economy and Competitiveness that supported TALISMAN+ (TIN2010-20510) research results detailed in this paper.

References

1. World Health Organization: Active Ageing. A Policy Framework. Second United Nations World Assembly on Ageing, Madrid, Spain (2002)
2. Cheek, P., Nikpour, L., Nowlin, H.D.: Aging Well With Smart Technology. Nursing Administration Quarterly 29(4), 329–338 (2005)
3. Williams, G., Doughty, K., Bradley, D.A.: A Systems Approach to Achieving CarerNet—An Integrated and Intelligent Telecare System. IEEE Transactions on Information Technology in Biomedicine 2(1), 1–9 (1998)
4. Laiseca, X., Castillejo, E., Orduña, P., Gómez-Goiri, A., López-de-Ipiña, D., González Aguado, E.: Distributed Tracking System for Patients with Cognitive Impairments. In: Bravo, J., Hervás, R., Villarreal, V. (eds.) IWAAL 2011. LNCS, vol. 6693, pp. 49–56. Springer, Heidelberg (2011)
5. Chen, L., Hoey, J., Nugent, C.D., Cook, D.J., Yu, Z.: Sensor-based Activity Recognition. IEEE Transactions on Systems, Man, and Cybernetics, Part C: Applications and Reviews 42(6), 790–808 (2012)
6. Docksteader, L., Benlamri, R.: MORF: A Mobile Health-Monitoring Platform. IT Professional 12(3), 18–25 (2010)
7. Cardinaux, F., Bhowmik, D., Abhayaratne, C., Hawley, M.S.: Video based technology for ambient assisted living: A review of the literature. Journal of Ambient Intelligent Smart Environments 3(3), 253–269 (2011)
8. Islam, K., Shen, W., Wang, X.: Security and Privacy Considerations for Wireless Sensor Networks in Smart Home Environments. In: Proceedings of the IEEE 16th International Conference on Computer Supported Cooperative Work in Design, pp. 626–633 (2012)
9. Gass, O., Maedche, A.: Enabling End-user-driven Data Interoperability – A Design Science Research Project. AMCIS 2011 Proceedings - All Submissions, paper 221 (2011)
10. Villarreal, V., Bravo, J., et al.: Towards Ubiquitous Mobile Monitoring for Health-care and Ambient Assisted Living. In: International Workshop on Ambient Assisted Living, Valencia, Spain (2010)
11. Chaaraoui, A., Climent, P., Flórez, F.: A Review on Vision Techniques applied to Human Behaviour Analysis for Ambient–Assisted Living. Expert Systems with Applications (in press), http://dx.doi.org/10.1016/j.eswa.2012.03.005
12. Balta-Ozkan, N., et al.: Social barriers to the adoption of smart homes. Energy Policy (2013), http://dx.doi.org/10.1016/j.enpol.2013.08.043
13. Cingolani, P., Alcalá-Fdez, J.: jFuzzyLogic: a Java Library to Design Fuzzy Logic Controllers According to the Standard for Fuzzy Control Programming. International Journal of Computational Intelligence Systems 6 (supp. 1) (2013)

Mobile Based Prompted Labeling
of Large Scale Activity Data

Ian Cleland[1], Manhyung Han[2], Christopher Nugent[1], Hosung Lee[2],
Shuai Zhang[1], Sally McClean[3], and Sungyoung Lee[2]

[1] Computer Science Research Institute and School of Computing and Mathematics,
University of Ulster, Newtownabbey, Co. Antrim, Northern Ireland, BT37 0QB
`{i.cleland,cd.nugent,s.zhang}@ulster.ac.uk`
[2] Dept. of Computer Engineering, Kyung Hee University, Korea
`{smiley,hslee,sylee}@oslab.khu.ac.kr`
[3] Computer Science Research Institute and School of Computing and Information Engineering,
University of Ulster, Coleraine, Northern Ireland, BT52 1SA
`si.mcclean@ulster.ac.uk`

Abstract. This paper describes the use of a prompted labeling solution to obtain
class labels for user activity and context information on a mobile device. Based
on the output from an activity recognition module, the prompt labeling module
polls for class transitions from any of the activities (e.g. walking, running) to
the standing still activity. Once a transition has been detected the system
prompts the user, through the provision of a message on the mobile phone, to
provide a label for the last activity that was carried out. This label, along with
the raw sensor data is then stored locally prior to being uploaded to cloud
storage. The paper provides technical details of how and when the system
prompts the user for an activity label and discusses the information that can be
gleaned from sensor data. This system allows for activity and context
information to be collected on a large scale. Data can then be used within new
opportunities in data mining and modeling of user context for a variety of
applications.

1   Introduction

The ubiquitous nature of smart phones within our everyday lives provides new
opportunities to collect real time context information, such as activity, location and
social interactions, from a large number of users [1]. This large amount of data has the
potential to be used in a number of application areas such as activity promotion, self
management of long term chronic health conditions, context aware services and life
logging [2]. The automatic recognition of activities is performed through the
application of machine learning techniques to data gleaned from low level sensors [3].
The training of these algorithms, from a data driven perspective, relies largely on the
gathering, pre-processing, segmentation and annotation of the sensor data into distinct
classes [4]. The data must therefore be correctly labeled prior to being used as a
training set in a machine learning paradigm.

C. Nugent, A. Coronato, and J. Bravo (Eds.): IWAAL 2013, LNCS 8277, pp. 9–17, 2013.
© Springer International Publishing Switzerland 2013

Collecting this data from a larger population under free living conditions may have the potential to improve the generalization abilities of any activity recognition (AR) models developed through provision of a larger quantity of representative data for training purposes. Such data sets should include data from a variety of sensors, recorded during a wide range of activities and contexts from a large number of users, over an extended period of time (months or years). Most importantly the data should also include accurate ground truth labels that represent user activities [5].

The use of smart phones can be viewed as one possible manner in which this large amount of data may be captured unobtrusively. Many handsets now have a range of in-built sensors, large memory storage, fast processing and low power communications, which meet the requirements of the range of data to be collected [6]. Furthermore, unlike many devices used as part of a research study, many potential subjects already own mobile phones, are accustomed to carrying them and always keep them charged [1]. Unfortunately, using mobile devices to gather data on a large scale can also prove difficult. In particular the integrity of the user annotation can be questionable. For example, users may forget to label a section of valuable data or may complete the labeling inaccurately. Nevertheless, a large scale fully annotated data set is recognised as being the key step to improve and increase the widespread adoption of AR applications [1], [6].

This paper presents an overview of a mobile based prompted labeling application aimed at overcoming the challenges associated with collecting annotated activity data on a large scale. In order to set the context of this work, a brief review of related material is presented. Following this the system architecture of the proposed prompt labeling application is described and the paper concludes with a discussion of the data which can be collected and analyzed.

2   Background

Although a large amount of research has focused on the ability to accurately detect a range of physical activities, very few studies have provided a detailed description of how the ground truth of data sets, for the purposes of a data driven approach to AR, have been acquired. To date the majority of AR studies have used data collected under structured or semi structured conditions, from a small number of participants (1-20 subjects). Participants often perform a set of preplanned tasks which are completed within a controlled environment [7], [8], [9], [10]. In this case, the ground truth is often recorded by a human observer and sensor data are then annotated offline according to the observer. This is viewed as being necessary as it allows researchers to capture the ground truth, when labeling data, in an effort to create highly accurate data sets. Data collected in this manner may not, however, be truly representative of completing the task in a free living environment. Furthermore, labeling and processing data is this manner can be a laborious and time consuming task for researchers. Boa and Intillie asked participants to complete a list of planned activities and to note the time at which they started and completed each activity [8]. Again this process of continuously noting the time at which an activity is commenced and completed is fine for short term laboratory based studies, however, would not be feasible in the long term under free living conditions.

In order to allow the collection of data in a more free living environment, researchers have utilized video cameras [11]. The subsequent video recording is reviewed offline to identify what activity was being performed at a particular time. Similar techniques have been used within smart environments to label the onset/ completion of object interactions [12]. Using groups of labelers sourced from the crowd is viewed as one way of dealing with the labour intensity of the task. Lasecki *et al.* [13] used activity labels, generated by groups of crowd sourced labelers to annotate activities from video data. All of the aforementioned labeling methods are labor intensive and time consuming and some approaches, in particular video annotation, can have implications with data privacy. Furthermore, the need to install or issue video cameras for recoding the activities reduces the scalability of the approach.

Alternatively on a larger scale, users are often asked to annotate their own data using a mobile interface. This usually requires the user to start and stop the data capture process manually [14]. When using the application the user is then asked to label the activity they have just or are about to complete. Although this method is relatively accurate at segmenting the activity it requires the user to explicitly start and stop recording. Tapia *et al.* [15] used a technique based on the experience sampling method to trigger self reported diary entries every 15 minutes. Multiple choice questions were answered by the user to select which of the 35 activities users were completing. Due to the intermittent nature of the labels it was found to be difficult to detect short time activities. The process of continually labeling can become laborious for users, particularly when performed over an extended period of time. Furthermore, this can result in the user providing incorrect labels for the data or simply not engaging with the system at all. In order for the user to input a label, some interaction with the mobile device is required. This may interrupt the user during the activity, which in turn may impact upon the activity that the person is undertaking, thus impacting overall on the data recorded. In an attempt to address the issue of interaction voice recognition has been used for the purposes of annotation [16]. The mobile device listens for key words such as "start activity" and "stop activity" to start and stop the recording. Voice recognition is then used to label the activity, with the user again saying keywords, such as "standing" or "walking". Nevertheless, having the smart phone continuously listening for keywords can consume battery power and may hamper the usability of the application. Additionally, inaccuracies of voice recognition can lead to mislabeling of data.

Our approach uses prompted labeling, driven by an underlying mobile based AR module, in an effort to improve the process of collecting and annotating data. Users can annotate their everyday activities through use of a personalized mobile application. When the user is detected as standing still, a prompt is provided to enable the user to label the activity they were previously completing. In this manner the sensor data for the respective activity is segmented and saved automatically and an activity label is supplied by the user after the activity has been finished thus maintaining the integrity of the data.

3   Prompted Data Labeling

The proposed mobile application is based upon the principle of prompts to label a user's context and activity data. At periodic times throughout the day, the application will prompt the user to confirm which activities they have just completed. In addition to user reported data, additional information gleaned from the mobile device, such as automated activity classifications, GPS latitude and longitude, accelerometry data and bluetooth interactions will also be recorded. This additional data will aid in further contextualizing the annotated data sets with the intention of improving the validity of labelling. An overview of the system architecture of the proposed application is shown in Fig. 1.

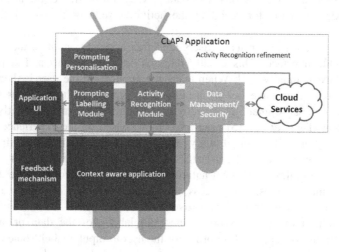

Fig. 1. An overview of personalized mobile application for prompt labelling. The prompted labeling module sits on top of an existing activity recognition module and periodically prompts users to label their activity. The architecture includes mobile services to support the secure transmission and processing of data in addition to the collection of other sensory data available from the mobile platform.

In order to enhance user engagement and compliance of the application it is important that the prompted labeling module is to be incorporated within an application which provides some incentive through appropriate feedback mechanisms. This type of application could include any context aware application such as an activity monitor, calorie counter or context aware services. A suite of mobile services will be developed to ensure the secure processing and transmission of all data collected from the users. These services will be responsible for managing security, efficient transmission of data and interfacing with cloud services. A brief description of these components is provided in Table 1.

Table 1. Provides a description of the main components of the system architecture

Component Name	Component Description
Prompt labeling module	This component contains a splash screen which allows the user to select a label for their activity data from a predefined list.
Activity recognition module	The activity recognition module attempts to detect changes in activity class to the standing still activity. From this a prompt is then initiated.
Data management	This module ensures the data is appropriately structured and formatted to ensure efficient transfer and storage. In this respect the security of the sensitive data is crucial, therefore efficient cryptography protocols shall be employed.
Cloud services	Cloud services provide the appropriate infrastructure to support data storage analysis and mining of the large data set.
Context aware application	The prompter sits upon a context aware application which enhances user engagement by providing tailored feedback (e.g. activity levels, calorie counting and context aware services)

3.1 Activity Recognition Module

The AR model used within this work, originally developed by Han *et al.* [17], utilizes multimodal sensor data from accelerometery, audio, GPS and Wi-Fi to classify a range of everyday activities such as walking, jogging and using transport. The activity recognition is performed independently of the position or orientation of the smart phone. This approach increases the practicality and usability of the system as the phone can be carried at any location and the AR is not affected by the user interacting with the device. Data from the accelerometer is used to detect transitions between ambulatory activities to activities which involve the use of transport. Accelerometer data, sampled at 50Hz, is computed into time and frequency domain features which are used as inputs to a Gaussian Mixture Classifier. Audio data is used in the classification if there is a need to classify between transportation activities (riding a bus or subway). Only using the audio when necessary allows the power consumption on the Smartphone to be minimized. GPS and Wi-Fi signals are then used to validate the classification between activities. Speed information, derived from GPS is used to determine whether a user is walking, running or standing still. The Wi-Fi signal is used to differentiate between bus and subway activities, as very few public or private wireless networks are available within the subway system.

3.2 Prompted Labeling Module

The prompted labeling module (PLM) prompts the user to label the activity they have just completed. Based on the output from the AR module the PLM polls for class transitions from any of the activities (e.g. walking and running) to the standing still activity. Once a transition has been detected the PLM prompts the user, through the provision of a message on the mobile phone, to provide a label for the last activity that was carried out. The raw data from the accelerometry sensors are then stored to the mobile device before being transmitted to the cloud for storage and further processing. By prompting the user to label the activity it is possible to verify that the activity has been correctly identified by the AR module. In this way the trustworthiness of the AR module can be validated in addition to providing a fully annotated data set. Fig. 2 presents an example of interaction with the prompt labeling screen on the mobile device.

Fig. 2. An example of user interaction with the prompt labeling screen. The AR module detects a change in class from the original activity to standing still. The prompt is then issued for the user to label the previous activity. Raw sensor data, for this activity, is then saved to the mobile device before being uploaded to the cloud for further processing and storage.

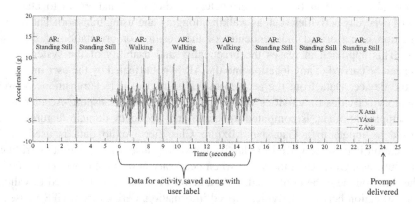

Fig. 3. Illustrates how activities are detected from the raw accelerometer signal by the AR module. Activates are detected every 3 seconds, three consecutive detections are used to label the activity. The prompt is initiated when the AR module detects a change in class from one activity to standing still.

The AR module detects an activity based on three seconds (150 samples) of data. Three consecutive detections (9 seconds) are then used to label the activity. This is carried out in order to limit the number of detection errors. Once the AR module detects a change from the current activity to the standing still activity for 9 seconds the previous activity data from the sensors is saved to memory. This process, from the perspective of raw accelerometry data is shown in Fig. 3. Currently, the prompt is initiated every time the AR detects a transition from an activity to standing still. It is envisioned that when the application is rolled out on a larger scale the user will be able to set how many prompts they receive per day in order to improve adoption of the system.

Currently data recorded by the system is stored directly to the local memory of the Smartphone, in the form of a text file. Fig. 4 shows the structure of this file. Data includes date and time stamp, raw accelerometer values (X, Y and Z axis), GPS latitude and longitude in addition to the Class label from the AR module and the prompted user label (named AR Label and User Label respectively). It is envisioned that this data could then be encrypted before being transmitted and stored in the cloud.

Date/ Time	Sample No.	Accel (X axis)	Accel (Y axis)	Accel (Z axis)	GPS (Lat)	GPS (Long)	AR Label	User label
201306141415	1	-5.152806193	3.587482	2.759922	54.68812	-5.88404	Walking	Walking
201306141415	2	-1.186659648	1.129002	-4.368226	54.68812	-5.88404	Walking	Walking
201306141415	3	-1.186659648	1.129002	-4.368226	54.68812	-5.88404	Walking	Walking
201306141415	4	0.886066667	3.421133	1.504522	54.68812	-5.88404	Walking	Walking
201306141415	5	0.886066667	3.421133	1.504522	54.68812	-5.88404	Walking	Walking
201306141415	6	2.60190622	1.719733	2.988136	54.68812	-5.88404	Walking	Walking
201306141415	7	1.487437767	0.281056	-0.683005	54.68812	-5.88404	Walking	Walking
201306141415	8	1.487437767	0.281056	-0.683005	54.68812	-5.88404	Walking	Walking
201306141415	9	-0.170149054	0.3915	-2.339131	54.68812	-5.88404	Walking	Walking
201306141415	10	-0.170149054	0.3915	-2.339131	54.68812	-5.88404	Walking	Walking
201306141415	11	-0.267032794	-0.10193	-1.685765	54.68812	-5.88404	Walking	Walking
201306141415	12	-0.267032794	-0.10193	-1.685765	54.68812	-5.88404	Walking	Walking
201306141415	13	0.163866438	-0.77931	-0.574205	54.68812	-5.88404	Walking	Walking
201306141415	14	0.163866438	-0.77931	-0.574205	54.68812	-5.88404	Walking	Walking
201306141415	15	0.288782327	-0.25574	0.478368	54.68812	-5.88404	Walking	Walking
201306141415	16	0.288782327	-0.25574	0.478368	54.68812	-5.88404	Walking	Walking
201306141415	17	0.667406954	0.356161	0.643228	54.68812	-5.88404	Walking	Walking
201306141415	18	0.667406954	0.356161	0.643228	54.68812	-5.88404	Walking	Walking
201306141415	19	0.061443988	0.43449	0.824545	54.68812	-5.88404	Walking	Walking
201306141415	20	0.061443988	0.43449	0.824545	54.68812	-5.88		
201306141415	21	0.295442565	0.464337	1.710036	54.6			
201306141415	22	1.423894523	-0.41485	1.54				
201306141415	23	1.423894523	-0.41					

Fig. 4. Shows an example of data recorded by the prompted labeling module. Recorded data includes, Date and time stamp, sample number, Accelerometer data from each axis, GPS latitude and longitude, in addition to the Class label from the AR module and prompted user label.

4   Summary

The ability to collect contextual information, such as activity, location or social interactions, on a large scale is becoming increasingly important. Such data sets allow for a deeper understanding of a population's activity habits and allow information to be delivered in a context sensitive manner. Current methods of collecting contextual information, particularly activity data, are normally limited to small scale studies. This is partly due to issues surrounding the ability to obtain ground truth information to annotate such data. The current approach aims to address such issues, through the use of a mobile based context aware PLM which prompts the user to supply label information for their current activities. In turn this improves the validity of data labels, which can then be used to improve the accuracy of data driven activity models. Transmitting and storing this data within the cloud opens new possibilities to exploit cloud services in order to mine these big data sets further in order to provide a deeper understanding of activity trends within healthcare. Plans for future work involve the evaluation of the current solution in order to assess its ability to accurately label data in a free living environment.

Acknowledgement. The authors wish to acknowledge support from the EPSRC through the MATCH programme (EP/F063822/1 and EP/G012393/1). The views expressed are those of the authors alone.

References

1. Intille, S.S., Lester, J., Sallis, J.F., et al.: New Horizons in Sensor Development. Medicine & Science in Sports & Exercise 44, S24–S31 (2012)
2. Hamm, J., Stone, B., Belkin, M., Dennis, S.: Automatic Annotation of Daily Activity from Smartphone-Based Multisensory Streams. In: Uhler, D., Mehta, K., Wong, J.L. (eds.) MobiCASE 2012. LNICST, vol. 110, pp. 328–342. Springer, Heidelberg (2013)
3. Preece, S.J., Goulermas, J.Y., Kenney, L.P.J., et al.: Activity Identification using Body-Mounted sensors—a Review of Classification Techniques. Physiol. Meas. 30, R1–R33 (2009)
4. Avci, A., Bosch, S., Marin-Perianu, M., et al.: Activity Recognition using Inertial Sensing for Healthcare, Wellbeing and Sports Applications: A Survey, pp. 1–10 (2010)
5. Hossmann, T., Efstratiou, C., Mascolo, C.: Collecting Big Datasets of Human Activity One Checkin at a Time, pp. 15–20 (2012)
6. Lane, N.D., Miluzzo, E., Lu, H., et al.: A Survey of Mobile Phone Sensing. IEEE Communications Magazine 48, 140–150 (2010)
7. Krishnan, N.C., Colbry, D., Juillard, C., et al.: Real Time Human Activity Recognition using Tri-Axial Accelerometers, pp. 1–5 (2008)
8. Bao, L., Intille, S.S.: Activity Recognition from User-Annotated Acceleration Data. In: Ferscha, A., Mattern, F. (eds.) PERVASIVE 2004. LNCS, vol. 3001, pp. 1–17. Springer, Heidelberg (2004)
9. Parkka, J., Ermes, M., Korpipaa, P., et al.: Activity Classification using Realistic Data from Wearable Sensors. IEEE Transactions on Information Technology in Biomedicine 10, 119–128 (2006)
10. Mannini, A., Intille, S.S., Rosenberger, M., et al.: Activity Recognition using a Single Accelerometer Placed at the Wrist Or Ankle. Med. Sci. Sports Exerc. (2013); E-Published ahead of Print
11. Plotz, T., Chen, C., Hammerla, N.Y., et al.: Automatic Synchronization of Wearable Sensors and Video-Cameras for Ground Truth Annotation–A Practical Approach, pp. 100–103 (2012)
12. Cruciani, F., Donnelly, M.P., Nugent, C.D., Parente, G., Paggetti, C., Burns, W.: DANTE: A video based annotation tool for smart environments. In: Par, G., Morrow, P. (eds.) S-CUBE 2010. LNICST, vol. 57, pp. 179–188. Springer, Heidelberg (2011)
13. Lasecki, W.S., Song, Y.C., Kautz, H., et al.: Real-Time Crowd Labeling for Deployable Activity Recognition, pp. 1203–1212 (2013)

14. Kawaguchi, N., Watanabe, H., Yang, T., et al.: HASC2012corpus: Large Scale Human Activity Corpus and its Application (2012)
15. Tapia, E.M., Intille, S.S., Larson, K.: Activity recognition in the home using simple and ubiquitous sensors. In: Ferscha, A., Mattern, F. (eds.) PERVASIVE 2004. LNCS, vol. 3001, pp. 158–175. Springer, Heidelberg (2004)
16. Harada, S., Lester, J., Patel, K., et al.: VoiceLabel: Using Speech to Label Mobile Sensor Data, pp. 69–76 (2008)
17. Han, M., Lee, Y., Lee, S.: Comprehensive Context Recognizer Based on Multimodal Sensors in a Smartphone. Sensors 12, 12588–12605 (2012)

Mobile NFC vs Touchscreen Based Interaction: Architecture Proposal and Evaluation

Pablo Curiel, Koldo Zabaleta, and Ana B. Lago

Deusto Institute of Technology - DeustoTech
MORElab – Envisioning Future Internet
University of Deusto, Avda. Universidades 24, 48007 - Bilbao, Spain
{pcuriel,koldo.zabaleta,anabelen.lago}@deusto.es

Abstract. The advances in ICTs have been significant during the last years, but progress in this area has not been accompanied by so significant improvements in user experience techniques. This has led to a certain group of people being unable to make use and benefit from the advanced features and services offered by these technologies. One of the most innovative technologies for human-computer interaction is the Near Field Communication (NFC). In this paper we present a platform that uses NFC technology in order to reduce the digital gap for mobile users, together with an experiment carried out with the goal of evaluating the differences between executing mobile services using the proposed platform and using the traditional touchscreen-based interaction.

Keywords: NFC, accesibility, mobile interaction, semantic technologies.

1 Introduction

The advances in information and communication technologies (ICT) have been significant during the last years. As an example, the speed of processors has been multiplied and the number of electronic devices with increased computing capabilities (smartphone, tablets, ...) has significantly increased. But progress in these aspects has not been accompanied by significant improvements in user experience techniques. This has led to a certain group of people being unable to make use and benefit from the advanced features and services offered by these technologies, as their technological skills and knowledge are not enough for doing so. Even people who are accustomed to technological advances have problems when running certain actions with their cell phone that could easily run before the smartphones were created. This phenomenon is known as the digital gap.

The user interfaces of these devices are one of the main causes of this digital gap, as they have not been designed for all kinds of users. For instance, many users have great difficulties accessing the functionalities of their mobile phones because the screen menus are very complex for them.

One of the most innovative technologies for human-computer interaction is the Near Field Communication (NFC), which we believe may be useful for reducing the digital gap. NFC is a combination of contactless identification and

C. Nugent, A. Coronato, and J. Bravo (Eds.): IWAAL 2013, LNCS 8277, pp. 18–25, 2013.

interconnection technologies that enable short-range wireless communications between mobile devices, consumer electronics, personal computers and smart objects. Based on this technology we propose a platform capable of executing the appropriate service or action depending on the tags read by the user.

In this paper we present both the NFC-based platform created in order to reduce the digital gap and the experiment carried out with the goal of evaluating the differences between executing mobile services using our platform and using a traditional touch-based application.

The remaining of this paper is structured as follows. The following section discusses related work. Section 3 gives a generic description of the platform. Section 4 describes the experiment carried out to compare the interaction model provided by our NFC-based platform to the default touchscreen-based one. Finally, in Section 5, conclusions and future work are exposed.

2 Related Projects

Up to date there have been several studies in which mobile phones equipped with NFC readers have been used to simplify the interaction with them and provide different services, following the Touch me paradigm [1].

The SmartTouch project [5] explores the NFC/RFID based interaction to provide new and innovative mobile services to the user. The goal of the platform is to provide users with the added value of interacting with intelligent objects in the environment in a simple and natural way.

Riekki et al. [3] propose a framework for requesting pervasive services touching RFID tags, in an attempt to connect the physical and digital world. They propose two types of tags: the general ones, which identify various objects in the environment (e.g. a printer), and the special ones, which are also linked to objects in the environment and represent additional information, actions and services that these objects can provide (e.g. print). Moreover, apart from the information contained in the RFID tags the framework uses the user context to select the most appropriate service to activate in each case.

REACHeS (Remotely Enabling and Controlling Heterogeneous Services) [4] is a framework which facilitates the activation of multimedia services (interactive catalogue, video player and slideshow viewer) combining mobile phones and NFC technology. Although services are activated using NFC tags, the actions over them (Pausing a video, showing next slide ...) must be done using screen menus.

Broll et al. [2] present a framework that provides access to semantic web services through what they call "physical mobile interaction". Thus, they have created physical objects augmented with technologies like RFID or QR codes. This augmented objects work as identifiers of services and input arguments for them, making the interaction with those services more intuitive.

Based in the reviewed projects, the goal of the solution proposed in this article is to simplify access to the new technologies through a NFC-based interface. In the existing solutions each service can been executed using only one NFC tag. As an extension of this method we use the idea of Broll et al. in which apart from the tags that identify proposed services other tags are used to determine the input parameters for them. However, in our proposal a tag represents an object, entity or action from the real world, not a service. And the combination of the read tags is what determines the service to be provided.

3   The Platform Infrastructure

In this paper we propose a platform that activates the most used services on mobile devices, such as making a call, by interacting with NFC tags. Thus, depending on the combination of tags users read, the system will recognize the service to activate and the parameters needed for its execution. With this work not only do we want to create a platform to help certain sectors of the population such as the elderly, but we also want everyone to have the possibility of running the actions offered by smartphones in a simpler and faster way.

The platform has been designed following a client-server architecture. The client side is an application for Android mobile devices which enables users to read NFC tags and executes the actions that correspond. The server is responsible for identifying the action to execute depending on the tags read by the user. The other axis of the platform is the model used to represent real world entities in NFC tags, which is paramount to recognize the action the user wants to execute. In the remainder of this section the features of these three main components are explained in more detail.

3.1   Model

To represent entities and objects using NFC tags and to define the actions that combinations of those determine, a formal representation model is required. We have used semantic web technologies like OWL ontologies for this purpose, a widely used approach for modelling real-world entities as well as making statements and reasoning about them. Thus, objects which can be represented in tags are modelled in an ontology hierarchy, as well as the actions to execute, which are a combination of different number and types of tags. Table 1 shows the actions the platform currently supports together with their object compositions.

Must be noted that, if in the future there is a need to add more actions, the only existing requirement is to create new Action classes which define its combination of Objects and its cardinality restrictions, as well as those new Object classes that the new Actions are comprised of.

3.2   Server

The server is responsible for inferring the action the mobile device must perform taking into account the set of tags selected by the user. For this purpose we use a combination of a semantic reasoner and a rule engine, which take the objects represented by the read tags as input and produce the right action to execute as output. For this reasoning, a rule-per-action design is adopted, in which each

Table 1. Actions with its tags and cardinality

Action	Objects
Read Email	1 ReadOutTag + 1 EmailTag
Send Email	1 EmailTag + 1-n Contact
Telephone Call	1 TelephoneTag + 1 Contact
See Photos	1 PhotoTag + 1 Contact
Show Weather Forecast	1 WeatherTag + 0-1 Addresable
See News	1 NewsTag + 1 InfoSource
Share Info	1 ShareTag + 1-n Contact

rule defined is responsible for checking if the conditions (i.e. the tags read) for its action are fulfilled. This way, in case more actions want to be supported, defining a new rule is only needed, regardless of the rules and actions existing before.

Although the server only offers this single functionality, its existence is essential because even if the inference task it carries out is not too computationally demanding for a traditional computer, currently there is no semantic reasoner capable of doing so in mobile devices within an acceptable response time.

3.3 Mobile Application

The mobile application has two separate though related functions. On the one hand, it provides users with the means to create the objects that make up the services and write them into NFC tags, and on the other hand it enables them to execute those actions or services by reading the tags.

To enable service provision to users when they read NFC tags, these tags must have been previously written with certain information that identifies each of them as a specific object or entity. Thus, the mobile application offers the possibility of managing all the tags users have. When users want to represent, for instance, a contact in a tag, the application enables them to select a contact in the phone agenda. Having it selected, the application creates an ontological instance representing this contact, stores it in a triplestore inside the mobile phone and writes its URI in the NFC tag. Later, when the user reads tags to execute certain action, the URIs of the entities represented in them are used to retrieve their instances from the triplestore. Those instances are sent to the server, which executes the rule engine an returns the action to execute to the mobile application, which finally executes it.

4   Touchscreen vs NFC Evaluation

In order to validate our proposal and to assess its convenience as an alternative to traditional touch interfaces, we carried out an interaction study. NFC is presented as a technology with potential to make interaction faster, easier and more comfortable for the end-users. Therefore, in this study we required subjects to execute three different actions both with the NFC-based interaction enabled by our platform and with a touch-based GUI. These actions were selected as representative of different interaction schemes. Therefore we had an action with no arguments, checking the weather forecast in the user's current location, an action with one argument, phoning a contact, and an action with two arguments, sending an e-mail to two contacts.

The interaction flow in those actions goes by as follows. In the NFC-based interaction, the user unlocks the mobile phone, reads the corresponding tags (see Table 1) and to finally execute the action touches the screen. This final screen tap is required, as is what the application understands as end-of-sequence to call the server to get the right action to execute. In the touch-based approach, the user begins unlocking the mobile phone, next starts the application with the shortcut in the home screen, then selects the 'Execute Action' option in the main menu and finally selects the action to execute and the corresponding arguments, if applicable (the contacts to call or send the e-mail). The user interface and the interaction flow for the touch-based part was explicitly designed for this evaluation, mimicking the NFC-based flow and its constrained options, in order to keep the comparison unbiased. For this reason the shortcut is placed in the home screen, enabling a fast application start, the action menu is limited to the three actions evaluated and the contact picking list is limited to two contacts, the same number of contact tags available in the NFC flow.

The experiment design was the following. First, we explained the purpose of the application to each subject. Next, by means of a live demo we introduced them to the application itself, how to read tags in the NFC-based interaction and to the user interface in the touch-based case. Then we asked them to execute the three actions with both interaction schemes, while the action execution times were automatically recorded by the application, since the user unlocked the mobile phone until each action successfully ended. In order to avoid a learning bias, half of the subjects were asked to execute first the three actions with NFC and the other half were asked to start with the touchscreen-based interface. Besides, we observed that the live demonstration of the application was not enough for all the subjects to get familiar with its functionality and some had doubts both with the graphical interface and the NFC tag reading. Therefore we extended the experiment with a second subject group which was requested to first execute some training actions in order to get comfortable with the application, enabling to research into the effect of this short training on task efficiency and the possible differences between both interaction approaches. Finally, after the actions execution, subjects were requested to answer a survey in order to record personal characteristics like age, sex or familiarity with both touchscreens and NFC technology, as well as subjective impressions towards the application.

The subject selection for the experiment was carried out asking for volunteers among the university staff, relatives and friends, so as to keep the sample varied in personal characteristics. In total, 40 subjects took part in the experiment. Subject age was between 20 and 60, with a right-skewed distribution of mean 35 and having three quarters of the subjects between 20 and 40 years old. The gender distribution was one quarter of women and three quarters of men. Regarding technological skills, measured with survey questions about computer and electronic device usage for everyday tasks, both subjects with low and high level of engagement participated in the study. However, the distribution is skewed to the left, with half of the subjects having a high technological engagement. On the other other hand, concerning familiarity with the technologies evaluated in the experiment, 4 out of 5 subjects are fully conversant with touchscreens, owning a mobile phone equipped with this kind of technology. In contrast, even though almost all subjects had used NFC or RFID technologies for different purposes like public transport passes, and about two thirds were familiar with the technology itself, only a third had actually used a NFC-enabled mobile phone. The subject training distribution was 15 subjects with prior training with the application and 25 with only a live demo of its functionality.

On to other terms, among the subjects taking part several dependencies were found between the mentioned characteristics, specially between subject age and others. First, an obvious correlation between age and technological skills can be observed. Thus, subjects under 40 years old have, in general, a great technological engagement. In contrast, older subjects, even if they own an smartphone or use computers for some regular tasks, show noticeable lower technological skills. Along that same line, there is a clear relationship between subject age and owning a touchscreen phone. This way, while all subjects under 40 have a touchscreen phone, only a third of the subjects over 40 own one. Similarly, there is an evident dependency between age and experience with NFC-enabled mobile devices, being all subjects with prior experience with one of these devices under 45 years old. Therefore, there is also an interaction between owning a touchscreen phone and subjects having experience with an NFC-enabled phone, as of all the seven subjects in the last group, only one has a non-touchscreen phone.

With respect to subjective impressions towards our NFC-based interaction proposal, the response was mainly positive. Nearly all subjects found this interaction approach useful (rating it at least 4 out of 6) and three quarters rated it 5 or 6 out of 6. Being asked whether they would use this application for everyday tasks, a quarter of the subjects answered that they would hardly or very occasionally use it, and the remaining three quarters evenly distributed between a frequent, very frequent and an everyday use.

Regarding task efficiency several conclusions can be drawn. Firstly, we can observe than on average NFC-based interaction is almost half a second faster than the touch-based one (7315 ms versus 7774 ms). Interaction times of actions executed with NFC are also less dispersed, with a standard deviation of around 4000 ms as opposed to 5000 ms in the case of those executed with the touchscreen. In the case of interaction times for each action type, these statistics are very similar. Thus, even if times differ (making a phone call takes more time than checking the weather forecast, as involves selecting more options), on average NFC-based approach is around 500 ms faster for the three actions. Looking at per-subject efficiency, 21 subjects were faster executing their tasks using NFC, as opposed to 19 subjects that were faster with the touch-based approach. This ratio is also maintained per action, having 64 actions executed faster with NFC, compared to 56 which took less time with the touchscreen-based interaction.

Studying the interaction between task efficiency and subject age, we can observe a significant linear correlation. This correlation is stronger for the actions executed with the touchscreen, being a one year increase in subject age associated with a 630 ms increase in action time (95% CI: 348 ms - 910 ms, P < 0.001). For NFC-based interaction a correlation can also be observed, which however is less significant and pronounced, being a one year increase in subject age associated with a 333 ms increase in action time (95% CI: 94 ms - 573 ms, P < 0.01). Besides, comparing interaction time differences (computed as touchscreen action times minus NFC action times for each subject) to subject age, a nice correlation can be observed. This way, a one year increase in subject age is associated with that subject being 300 ms faster with NFC than with a touchscreen (95% CI: 119 ms - 472 ms, P ≈ 0.001). Thus it can be noticed that in general younger subjects (less than 30 years old) are faster with the touch-based approach, while older ones are faster using NFC, as Fig. 1 shows.

Looking into the difference between touch-based actions executed by subjects owning a touchscreen phone and those who don't, we see a very significant correlation, being subjects without a touchscreen phone 18 seconds slower on average (95% CI: -27167 ms - -9341 ms, P < 0.001). Similarly, subjects with previous experience with NFC-enabled phones are faster in the NFC-based actions than those who hadn't previously used this type of interaction. However, the difference is smaller than in the previous case, around 6 seconds on average, and the correlation is not so significant (95% CI: -12507 ms - 492 ms, P ≈ 0.05), as it can be concluded observing Fig. 2.

Concerning the effect of the pre-experiment training on interaction times, subjects which trained were faster than those who didn't both with NFC and touchscreen interfaces. Concretely, subjects with training were on average 2 seconds faster executing the actions with both the NFC and the touch-based interfaces. Therefore both groups were on average faster with NFC.

Finally, comparing the subjective impressions of the subjects to task execution times no correlation is found. Thus, it can be concluded that they finding the NFC-based interaction useful or desirable has no relationship with they being faster with this interaction approach.

Summing up, we can extract the following two main conclusions from the experiment. The first one is that using NFC is a faster way for accessing the services provided by latest smartphones, specially for older people (over 30 years old), for those who are less familiar with touch-based interaction or for those less familiar with new technologies in general. The second conclusion is that learning to use an NFC-enabled phone is fast and the improvement is high (around 2 seconds for the tasks in the experiment). This hypothesis is supported by the interaction times difference between the group who had prior experience with NFC and the group who had not being relatively small.

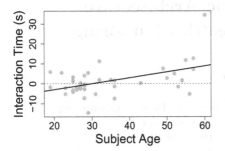

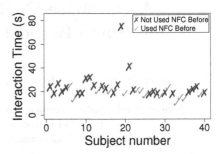

Fig. 1. Interaction times difference (Touchscreen - NFC) related to age

Fig. 2. Interaction times using NFC related to NFC Experience

5   Conclusion

In this article we have presented a platform to access the most-used services in mobile phones using NFC. In order to assess the convenience of this approach as an alternative to traditional touch interfaces, we have also presented a comparative study between these two technologies. This experiment has demonstrated that NFC is a convenient, easy to learn and comfortable way for interacting with mobile devices. NFC has also proved faster than the touch-based interaction, specially among older people and those with less technological skills.

However, it should be desirable to run a larger scale experiment, in which the distribution of the subjects taking part in it were more homogeneous, including more subjects in older age groups as well as more people with lower technological skills. Finally, in order to gain a better insight on the differences between NFC and touch-based interaction, a longer experiment would be required, in which subjects would be able to get more familiar with this interaction technologies, and in which capturing interaction errors could also be possible.

References

1. Ailisto, H., Matinmikko, T., Ylisaukko-Oja, A., Strommer, E., Hillukkala, M., Wallin, A., Siira, E., Poyry, A., Tormanen, V., Huomo, T.: Physical browsing with NFC technology. VTT (2007)
2. Broll, G., Siorpaes, S., Rukzio, E., Paolucci, M., Hamard, J., Wagner, M., Schmidt, A.: Supporting mobile service usage through physical mobile interaction. In: Fifth Annual IEEE International Conference on Pervasive Computing and Communications, PerCom 2007, pp. 262–271. IEEE (2007)
3. Riekki, J., Salminen, T., Alakarppa, I.: Requesting pervasive services by touching rfid tags. IEEE Pervasive Computing 5(1), 40–46 (2006)
4. Sánchez, I., Cortés, M., Riekki, J.: Controlling multimedia players using nfc enabled mobile phones. In: Proceedings of the 6th International Conference on Mobile and Ubiquitous Multimedia, MUM 2007, pp. 118–124. ACM, New York (2007)
5. SmartTouch: Browsing through smart objects around you (2006), http://ttuki.vtt.fi/smarttouch/www/?info=whatissmarttouch

A Database-Centric Architecture
for Home-Based Health Monitoring

Wagner O. de Morais, Jens Lundström, and Nicholas Wickström

School of Information Science, Computer and Electrical Engineering,
Halmstad University, Halmstad, Sweden
{wagner.demorais,jens.lundstrom,nicholas.wickstrom}@hh.se

Abstract. Traditionally, database management systems (DBMSs) have
been employed exclusively for data management in infrastructures
supporting Ambient Assisted Living (AAL) systems. However, DBMSs
provide other mechanisms, such as for security, dependability, and extensibility that can facilitate the development, use, and maintenance of AAL
applications. This work utilizes such mechanisms, particularly extensibility, and proposes a database-centric architecture to support home-based
healthcare applications. An active database is used to monitor and respond to events taking place in the home, such as bed-exits. In-database
data mining methods are applied to model early night behaviors of people
living alone. Encapsulating the processing into the DBMS avoids trans-
ferring and processing sensitive data outside of database, enables changes
in the logic to be managed on-the-fly, and reduces code duplication. As a
result, such an approach leads to better performance and increased security and privacy, and can facilitate the adaptability and scalability of AAL
systems. An evaluation of the architecture with datasets collected in real
homes demonstrated the feasibility and flexibility of the approach.

Keywords: Healthcare technology, ambient assisted living, active databases, in-database processing, machine learning.

1 Introduction

1.1 Background and Related Work

Over the past several years, there has been an increased interest in using the
pervasive infrastructure of smart homes to support Ambient Assisted Living
(AAL). The collection and analysis of functional, safety, security, and physiological parameters, as well as cognitive support, are the most common smart home
applications in healthcare [1]. In-home health monitoring provides accurate and
reliable long-term data to support better decision making, better understanding
of aging and illnesses, the prevention and management of chronic diseases, and
the conservation of healthcare resources [2]. Long-term storage enables the use
of data mining methods that can reveal patterns or unknown relationships that
describe, for example, the onset of a health-related problem [3].

C. Nugent, A. Coronato, and J. Bravo (Eds.): IWAAL 2013, LNCS 8277, pp. 26–34, 2013.
© Springer International Publishing Switzerland 2013

A number of smart home and AAL projects have been developed recently [4,5] along with technical infrastructures, such as UniversAAL [6], that serve as a foundation for AAL applications. Although some architectural aspects are common among existing smart homes and AAL platforms [7], there is still no widely adopted method for developing these systems. In fact, smart homes and AAL systems are still complex to build, use, and maintain [8]. One factor contributing to such complexity is the inherent diversity that is characteristic of smart homes. Individuals have needs and preferences that differ and evolve over time. Home environments also differ. In addition to the variety of home environments, heterogeneous technologies that operate on different standards are employed in these systems. The acceptance of AAL systems is directly linked with their capability to address an individual's evolving needs as well as privacy, security, and dependability concerns [9].

1.2 Approach and Contribution

In response to the challenges described above, this work presents a database-centric system architecture that exploits mechanisms provided by database management systems (DBMSs), other than data management, to support home-based healthcare applications. Modern DBMSs, such as PostgreSQL [10], are mature technologies and provide mechanisms that can be utilized to address important requirements for security, privacy, dependability, extensibility, and scalability in smart home and AAL systems. Such mechanisms have not been explored by current smart home and AAL infrastructures that employ DBMSs exclusively for data storage and retrieval. More specifically, this work utilizes the extensibility capabilities and the event-driven mechanisms supported by DBMSs to detect and respond to events taking place in the home environment within the database itself. Pushing the domain logic into the database reduces data communication and this leads to better performance and increased security and privacy because there is no need to export sensitive data outside the database [11]. DBMSs enable changes in the domain logic to be managed on-the-fly and this facilitates scalability because changes in software applications connected to the DBMS are not required. Current approaches typically implement the domain logic, as well as mechanisms for security, privacy, and dependability, at the application or middleware layers. Because storage is a

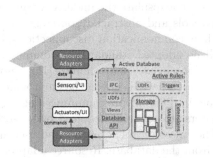

Fig. 1. The system architecture includes Resource Adapters and an Active Database

required functionality in continuous, long-term home-based monitoring systems, the DBMS is the most common, but not fully exploited, component among smart home and AAL platforms.

The remainder of this paper is organized as follows. The proposed approach is presented in Section 2. Section 3 describes the dataset that inspired the development of three home-based healthcare services demonstrating the proposed approach. The results and conclusions are covered in Sections 4 and 5, respectively.

2   Database-Centric System Architecture

DBMSs offer mechanisms known as active rules (triggers) that allow the database to detect and respond to events such as data manipulation operations (table insertions and updates). Databases exploiting active rules are called active databases [12]. In conjunction with sensors and actuators, active databases can monitor and react to events happening in the environment. DBMSs also allow developers to extend the query language (SQL) with user-defined functions (UDFs) that can encapsulate the semantics of applications, statistical models, and machine learning techniques. Together with database views, UDFs can be used to define a database API to hide the underlying database model. Database triggers, UDFs, and views are stored in the database and are managed on-the-fly without requiring system restarts. Software applications, called resource adapters, can be used to abstract and integrate heterogeneous hardware and software resources into the system. The main modules of the proposed architecture are illustrated in Fig. 1 and are further explained in later subsections.

2.1   Resource Adapters

Sensors and actuators provide the means for perceiving and controlling the environment. Resource adapters are software components in the architecture that abstract heterogeneous hardware (sensors and actuators) and software technologies (user interfaces and files) to facilitate their integration and interoperation into the system. Resource adapters resemble context widgets and context services [13] but with fewer responsibilities (no data aggregation or peer-to-peer communication). Adapters encapsulate the underlying implementation of different communication protocols and abstract resource specific data formats. Recovery from faults, such as communication disconnections, is also provided.

Because there is still no adopted standard for communicating and integrating devices and applications inside smart homes [14], resource adapters have been designed to serve as a gateway between the environment and the database and to be implementable in different programming languages, such as C# and Python. Resource adapters stream data acquired by sensors or entered by the user to the database. They also control actuators and user interfaces in response to commands received from the database. Resource adapters communicate with the database through a database API while the database employs interprocess communication mechanisms to communicate with resource adapters.

2.2 Active Database

The active database (Fig. 1) contains four main modules as follows.

Storage. This module includes tables storing sensor data and processed information and tables containing information of resources (sensors and actuators), such as their location, capabilities, and configuration. Developers implementing resource adapters do not have access to the internal Storage model. They are provided instead with a Database API.

Database API. The internal database model is hidden or protected by a Database API that exposes data access and manipulation (selections, insertions, and updates) using views and UDFs. To notify resource adapters about data changes or events, the database makes use of external or built-in mechanisms for interprocess communication. Such an approach avoids adapters from periodically querying (polling) the database. PostgreSQL provides the NOTIFY and LISTEN commands for interprocess communication.

Active Rules. An active database monitors and reacts to specific circumstances of relevance to an application in a timely manner [12]. The reactive behavior in an active database system is supported by Event-Condition-Action structures referred as active rules. When an event occurs, the condition is evaluated and if it holds an action is executed. In PostgreSQL, for example, active rules are implemented using triggers and UDFs. Periodic execution of database UDFs can be achieved with job scheduling utilities that are built into the DBMS or into the operating system.

Database Extensions. Advanced algorithms, such as methods for statistical analysis, can be integrated into modern DBMSs. For example, MADlib is an open-source library that adds in-database analytical capabilities to PostgreSQL. The library supports established machine learning methods such as Decision Trees (DTs), Random Forests, and Support Vector Machines [15]. In-database processing reduces the amount of code at the application level and avoids data transfers as described at the beginning of this section.

3 In-Database Services for Home-Based Healthcare Monitoring Using the "Trygg om natten" Dataset

The "Trygg om natten" ("Safe at night") dataset originated from a recent study conducted in Halmstad, Sweden, that explored how technology could assist care beneficiaries and caregivers during night supervisions [16]. The study also focused on how technology was perceived by the participants in terms of integrity and acceptance. In total, the homes of 15 care beneficiaries were equipped with five types of sensors (Table 1) that were active from 10 p.m. until 6 a.m. every

Table 1. Sensors used to collect the dataset [16]

Type	Purpose	Qty.	Output
Passive infrared (PIR)	Capture human motion	3-5	Binary
Quasi-electric film (EMFIT)	Capture bed exits	1	Binary
Magnetic	Capture door openings	1	Binary
Inertial sensor	Capture human inactivity (wearable)	1	Binary
Load cells	Reference to the EMFIT sensor	1	24-bit value

night during approximately 14 days. The study was granted with an ethical approval from the central ethical review board. One of the outcomes of the study was a set of requirements specifications for AAL services, particularly those related to nighttime caregiving. The following services have been inspired by the project [16].

Bed Presence or Absence Detection. This service can enable the night patrol team to remotely check if individuals are in bed so as not to disturb their sleep. Voluntary and involuntary body movements generate disturbances in the load cell signal that are not present when the bed is unoccupied or when it is loaded with static weight. By analyzing such signal variance, a method to detect the presence or absence of a person in bed can be implemented as an active rule (trigger) that monitors the table in which load cell signal values are stored. The condition for the active rule consists of checking intervals in which the standard deviation of the last 160 inserted samples ($\approx$2 seconds) is greater than a discriminating threshold. A method for finding this threshold in a signal (i.e. binarizing) is the Otsu algorithm [17] that maximizes the between cluster distance when dividing the distribution values into two clusters, for example, the in-bed and out-of-bed clusters. For each individual, a corresponding threshold is calculated.

Common Event Transitions during the Night. The purpose of this service is to discover simple associations between presence detections in rooms (bathroom and kitchen) and the bed. Strong associations indicate common room transitions and room activity, and deviations from such associations could enable the detection of anomalies. A method for finding such patterns in sequences of events (i.e. sequential data mining [18]) is by estimating the probability of one event being followed by another type of event (similarly to [19]), i.e. event e_x being followed by event e_y, $P(e_y|e_x)$. By considering only the previous detected event, a transition matrix can be computed online for each individual using an active rule. Each element in the transition matrix P contains the probability of event e_i being followed by event e_j and this is denoted as $P_{ij}(e_j|e_i)$, also referred to as *confidence* in association rules [20]. The transition matrix can be visualized as a graph by plotting associations over a certain confidence threshold.

Modeling of Early Night Behavior Using DTs. Another way to model transitions is with a service that models typical sensor triggering transitions over a certain time-span during the night. Such a service could help to discover changing trends in the level of independence of the individual being monitored. For this service, a DT was trained with data from a single individual to discriminate among two classes: the time period from 10 p.m. to midnight (TPI) and the period from midnight to 6 a.m. (!TPI). The training data consisted of 15 features that were computed for each observation by processing a sliding window with a width of 20 minutes over the 14 days of collected data. This process resulted in training data with approximately 300 observations. The events in the collected data are denoted as bathroom (**Ba**), kitchen (**K**), hallway (**H**), and living room (**L**), and each event represents activity in a certain room. Other events include inactivity registered from the wearable inertial sensor (**I**), door openings (**D**), and bed entrances and exits (**Bin** and **Bout**) that are computed from the load cell data. The features used in the calculations are the types of sensors that fired in the last four events and are denoted as *Event at time t*. The transition time between the four last events for a window is computed as $Et(t, t - k)$ where k is the number of previous events. The number of each type of event in the window is also computed, and the lack of events in a window is denoted by **N**.

4 Results

To accommodate the proposed architecture, a database server was configured in a computer running CentOS 6.4 with PostgreSQL (version 9.2.3) and the MADlib [15] library extension. To implement the proposed services, additional tables were created that stored temporary and derived data such as descriptive statistics and transition matrices. A separate computer running MS-Windows 7 hosted resource adapters (implemented in C#) that read and streamed measurements from the dataset files to the corresponding database. For simplification purposes, only one dataset from a single care beneficiary was selected to represent the results of the experiment.

Bed Presence or Absence Detection
For the selected individual, 27 bed presences and 16 bed absences were detected by the active rule. To identify true and false positives, the dataset containing load cell signals was manually labeled (27 bed-entrances and 16 bed-exits were identified based on the measured weight) and served as a baseline for comparison. All bed presence and absence detections were validated as true positives. Bed absence detections outnumbered bed presence detections because on many occasions the individual left the bed when the sensors were inactive after 6 a.m..

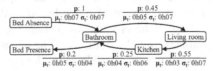

Fig. 2. Transition probabilities (p) of events for a confidence threshold of 0.2. Mean (μ_t) and standard deviation (σ_t) of the transition time (normally distributed)

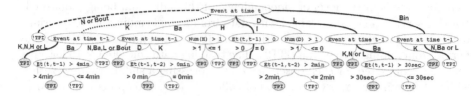

Fig. 3. A DT distinguishes different time periods during the night

Common Event Transitions during the Night. An active rule, which monitors incoming sensor events, updates the transition matrix table, which describes the transition probability of events happening during the night. The computation of statistics, such as the mean and standard deviation of the transition time between two events, are also triggered by the rule. Fig. 2 presents likely transitions of events in the home environment of the selected subject. An observation from the figure is that when the observed individual leaves the bed the most likely event is a visit to the bathroom. Such transition takes an average of 7 minutes with a standard deviation of 7 minutes. This knowledge provided by the transition matrix could be used to detect anomalies during future nights.

Modeling of Early Night Behavior Using DTs. For the same individual, the generated DT is shown in Fig. 3. Thick edges represent where the majority of data points were concentrated. One interpretation of the model is illustrated by the dashed edge from the root node. This link revealed that the individual was more likely to be active during the modeled time period TPI than the rest of the night (!TPI). Moreover, the dotted edge shows that the individual was active in the kitchen, hallway and living room during TPI. In order to validate the DT model, a 10-fold cross-validation was performed and a mean accuracy of 81% was achieved. The accuracy shows that, despite the complexity of human behavior, the model is able to explain key features of the early night that could be used when analyzing deviations in long-term trends.

5 Discussion and Conclusion

Databases are mature technologies and provide mechanisms that can address the security, privacy, dependability, extensibility, and scalability requirements of smart home and AAL systems. These mechanisms, however, are not fully exploited in current smart home and AAL infrastructures. This work proposes a database-centric architecture that utilizes database capabilities, such as extensibility, to facilitate the development of home-based healthcare applications. Resource adapters that abstract heterogeneous technologies can serve as gateways between the environment and the database. The event-driven architecture provided by active databases made it possible to implement a service within the database to monitor an individual's presence or absence in bed. Database extensions for data mining enabled the development of services to model early night behaviors. These services, which have been validated with a dataset collected in real homes, reside within the database and avoid exporting sensitive data to external data analysis tools. Such an approach leads to improved performance, security, and flexibility while benefiting from the management capabilities of DBMSs. Centralizing the domain logic into the DBMS reduces code duplication and facilitates the adaptability and scalability of the system as individual needs evolve. The database model is an ongoing work and aims to describe resources using semantic technologies to facilitate integration, adaptation, reasoning, and knowledge extraction.

Acknowledgments. The authors would like to thank all the participants in the project [16].

References

1. Demiris, G., Hensel, B.K.: Technologies for an aging society: a systematic review of "smart home" applications. In: Yearbook of Medical Informatics, pp. 33–40 (2008)
2. Kang, H.G., Mahoney, D.F., Hoenig, H., Hirth, V.A., et al.: In situ monitoring of health in older adults: Technologies and issues. Journal of the American Geriatrics Society 58(8), 1579–1586 (2010)
3. Rashidi, P., Cook, D.J.: Mining and monitoring patterns of daily routines for assisted living in real world settings. In: Proceedings of the 1st ACM International Health Informatics Symposium, pp. 336–345 (2010)
4. Chan, M., Estève, D., Escriba, C., Campo, E.: A review of smart homes - present state and future challenges. Computer Methods and Programs in Biomedicine 91(1), 55–81 (2008)
5. Rashidi, P., Mihailidis, A.: A survey on ambient-assisted living tools for older adults. IEEE Journal of Biomedical and Health Informatics 17(3), 579–590 (2013)
6. Tazari, M.R., Furfari, F., Valero, F., Hanke, S., et al.: The universAAL reference model for AAL. In: Handbook on Ambient Assisted Living-Technology for Healthcare, Rehabilitation and Well-being. AISE Book Series, vol. 11, pp. 610–625 (2012)
7. Fagerberg, G., et al.: Platforms for AAL applications. In: Lukowicz, P., Kunze, K., Kortuem, G. (eds.) EuroSSC 2010. LNCS, vol. 6446, pp. 177–201. Springer, Heidelberg (2010)
8. Eckl, R., MacWilliams, A.: Smart home challenges and approaches to solve them: A practical industrial perspective. In: Tavangarian, D., Kirste, T., Timmermann, D., Lucke, U., Versick, D. (eds.) IMC 2009. CCIS, vol. 53, pp. 119–130. Springer, Heidelberg (2009)
9. Demiris, G., Thompson, H.J., Reeder, B., Wilamowska, K., et al.: Using informatics to capture older adults wellness. Int. Journal of Medical Informatics (2011)
10. The PostgreSQL Global Development Group: Postgresql 9.2 documentation (2013)
11. Ordonez, C.: Data set preprocessing and transformation in a database system. Intelligent Data Analysis 15(4), 613–631 (2011)
12. Paton, N.W., Daz, O.: Active database systems. ACM Computing Surveys (CSUR) 31(1), 63–103 (1999)
13. Dey, A.K., Abowd, G.D., Salber, D.: A conceptual framework and a toolkit for supporting the rapid prototyping of context-aware applications. Human-Computer Interaction 16(2-4), 97–166 (2001)

14. Kim, J.E., Boulos, G., Yackovich, J., Barth, T., et al.: Seamless integration of heterogeneous devices and access control in smart homes. In: 2012 8th International Conference on Intelligent Environments (IE), pp. 206–213 (2012)
15. Hellerstein, J.M., Ré, C., Schoppmann, F., Wang, D.Z., Fratkin, E., et al.: The MADlib analytics library: or MAD skills, the SQL, vol. 5, pp. 1700–1711 (2012)
16. Thörner, R., Persson, M., Eriksson, H., Isaksson, A., Lundström, J.: Trygg om natten. Technical report, Centre for Health Technology in Halland, Halmstad University, Halmstad, Sweden (2011)
17. Otsu, N.: A threshold selection method from gray-level histograms. IEEE Transactions on Systems, Man and Cybernetics 9(1), 62–66 (1979)
18. Agrawal, R., Srikant, R.: Mining sequential patterns. In: Proceedings of the Eleventh International Conference on Data Engineering, pp. 3–14 (1995)
19. Guralnik, V., Haigh, K.Z.: Learning Models of Human Behaviour with Sequential Patterns. In: Proceedings of the AAAI 2002 workshop "Automation as Caregiver", pp. 24–30 (2002)
20. Agrawal, R., Imielinski, T., Swami, A.: Mining association rules between sets of items in large databases. ACM SIGMOD Record 22, 207–216 (1993)

Improving Health Services Using Cloud Computing, Big Data and Wireless Sensors

Diego Gachet Páez, Víctor Padrón , Manuel de Buenaga, and Fernando Aparicio

Universidad Europea de Madrid, 28670 Villaviciosa de Odón, Spain
{gachet,victor.padron,buenaga,fernando.aparicio}@uem.es

Abstract. In a society characterized by aging population and economical crisis it is desirable to reduce the costs of public healthcare systems. It is increasingly necessary to streamline the health system resources leading to the development of new medical services such as telemedicine, monitoring of chronic patients, personalized health services, creating new services for dependants, etc. Those new application and services will significantly increasing the volume of health information to manage, including data from medical and biological sensors, contextual information, health records, reference information, etc., which in turn requires the availability of health applications anywhere, at any time and also access to medical information must be pervasive and mobile. In this paper we propose one potential solution for creating those new services, especially in outdoors environments, based on cloud computing and vital signs monitoring.

Keywords: internet of things, cloud computing, elderly, sensors.

1   Introduction

At the present time, developed countries have great difficulties with effective management of health services and quality of care in a context marked by the population ageing and economical crisis. In Spain, for example, at the 2010 year there were 7.500.00 people over 65 years old, whereas in the 2020 this number will grow until the 9.000.000, this tendency that also is observable in all European countries, has dramatic effects on the public and private health systems including the emergencies service. At the other hand, in the last decades there exists an undeniable increase in chronic diseases [1].

Recent data of the European Union reveals the main chronic pathologies are the following ones: diabetes; according to International Diabetes Federation (IDF), the global cost of the diabetes in Europe was approximately of €68.300 million in 2007 and will grow until €80.900 millions in 2025 [2]. According to countries, depending on the prevalence and the level of available treatments, the cost in diabetes will be in a rank of 2.5 - 15% of the total of sanitary expenses. The cardiovascular diseases, including all the diseases of the circulatory system, demanded a total cost in Europe in 2006 of €109,000 million (10% of the total of the sanitary cost; in Spain 7%) [2]. Indirect costs include €41,000 million loss of productivity and €42,000 million of the

C. Nugent, A. Coronato, and J. Bravo (Eds.): IWAAL 2013, LNCS 8277, pp. 35–38, 2013.
© Springer International Publishing Switzerland 2013

cost of the informal cares. All it makes a total of €192,000 millions in 2006. Considering the above mentioned data it becomes necessary to create tools and technologies that enable the development of new health services for the elderly, chronics patients and dependent persons [3] [4], which in turn contribute to the sustainability of the health system.

2   Proposed Architecture for Chronic Patients Monitoring

The proposed technological architecture for chronic patient monitoring and dependant persons care, both outdoors and indoor as well as its associated services is presented in Figure 1.

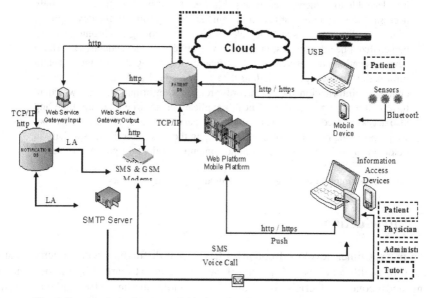

Fig. 1. Proposed Architecture for indoor /outdoor chronic patients monitoring

This architecture is being developed in the context of Virtual Cloud Carer project (VCC) [5] and consists of the following principal elements:

- A smart mobile device being used by chronics patients and dependent which in turn accepts the data from vital sign sensors and sends this information via the mobile network 3G/HDSPA. Due to large amount of data to be generated, the current general models based on common databases (mostly relational) are not sufficient, it's not that they are not required, they are simply not enough, if it is necessary to use Big Data technologies for store and process this information.
- A rule generation system for activation of alarms to be sent to the chronic patient's caregivers or nursing or medical personnel, by using the new technology of Cloud Computing.

- Interoperability and messaging platform for the delivery of information to all involved actors in the system, using the latest technological advances in communication (SMS, mail, voice automated systems and PUSH technology).
- A website platform that allows both social workers and family caregivers, consult the associated patient information from both a desktop computer and/or from mobile devices.
- A subsystem for generating rehabilitation exercises for elderly with mobility restrictions, based on 3D image recognition.
- A module for finding health-related information [6]; in this case the user can make use of a Web interface for searching using natural language medical terms related to their health status, his module gets information from various sources such as MedlinePlus [7] or FreeBase [8].

3   Smart Mobile Device and Sensors

The design of a mobile device to capture vital signs from sensors, should take into account the diversity of technologies and different communication protocols available today for interaction with the sensors and the Internet. At present time we are doing tests with a Bluetooth pulseoximeter and wired electrodes for detecting cardio respiratory diseases; the device allows taking sensor data with a configurable sampling frequency, filtering, storing and sending this information to the Internet, the prototype is based on a PIC 18F87J60, figure 2 shows the main components corresponding to a GPS unit, GSM unit, PIC microcontroller, Bluetooth module and power supply.

Fig. 2. 3D model for Smart mobile device

4   Conclusions and Future Work

The current health care systems are characterized of a number of deficiencies that prevent greater effectiveness in service. Some of these defects are for example: lack of reactivity, discontinuity in care service, saturation in emergency and consultation service, etc. We are convinced that Virtual Cloud Carer project could help to avoid those problems transforming the sanitary system in preventive, proactive, global and participative, maintaining a full control about patient's situation and a reasonably cost. During the last stage of the project, at end of year 2013, will running two case studies (scenarios) to demonstrate the functionality of the developed architecture, a scenario has to deal with home rehabilitation based on the motion recognition system, Internet access using adapted tools and voice commanded desktop applications, while another scenario will consist of a day care centre for elder people, who in turn can carry the mobile device with vital signs sensors, these scenarios will permit participation of users that can validate developed technology and to obtain their views and suggestions in the near future in order to commercialize project's results.

Acknowledgments. The Virtual Cloud Carer Project, described in this article, is being developed by the European University of Madrid, and the companies Cubenube and Encore that is the project coordinator; VCC has been partially funded by the Spanish Ministry of Industry, Tourism and Trade TSI-020100-2011-83 through Avanza2 R&D framework. Some modules have been partially funded by the Spanish Ministry of Science and Innovation under (TIN-2009-14057-C03-01) and Universidad Europea de Madrid under internal project ID 2013UEM03.

References

1. WHO global report. Preventing chronic diseases: a vital investment. World Health Organization (2005)
2. Fundación Vodafone. Innovación TIC para las personas mayores. Situación, requerimientosy atención integral de la cronicidad y la dependencia   (2011),   http://www.vodafone.es/static/fichero/pro_ucm_mgmt_015568.pdf
3. Burdick, D., Kuown, S.: Gerotechnology: Research and Practice in Technology and Aging, 1st edn. Springer Publishing Company (2004)
4. Wang, F., Docherty, L.S., Turner, K.J., Kolberg, M., Magill, E.H.: Service and policies for care at home. In: Proc. 1st Int. Conf. on Pervasive Computing Technologies for Healthcare, pp. 7.1–7.10. IEEE Press (November 2006)
5. Virtual Cloud Carer web Site, http://www.virtualcloudcarer.com
6. Gachet, D., Aparicio, F., Buenaga, M., Padrón, V.: Health Care System with Virtual Reality Rehabilitation and Appropriate Information for Seniors. Sensors 12(5), 5502–5516 (2012) ISSN 1424-8220
7. Medlineplus Web, http://www.nlm.nih.gov/medlineplus
8. López-Fernández, H., Reboiro-Jato, M., Glez-Peña, D., Aparicio, F., Gachet, D., Buenaga, M., Fdez-Riverola, F.: BioAnnote: A software platform for annotating biomedical documents with application in medical learning environments. Computer Methods and Programs in Biomedicine (2013)
9. Augusto, J.C.: Towards personalization of services and an integrated service model for smart homes applied to elderly. In: Proc. Int. Conf. on Smart Homes and Health Telematics, Sherbrooke, Canada, pp. 151–158 (July 2005)

Focus Group Evaluation of Scenarios for Fall Risk Assessment and Fall Prevention in Two Countries

Heidi Similä[1], Milla Immonen[1], Carlos García Gordillo[2],
Tuula Petäkoski-Hult[1], and Patrik Eklund[3]

[1] VTT Technical Research Centre of Finland, Finland
{heidi.simila,milla.immonen}@vtt.fi,
tuula.petakoski-hult@thh-palvelut.fi
[2] CGG Management, Spain
cgarcia.management@cemad.es
[3] Umeå University, Sweden
peklund@cs.umu.se

Abstract. Information and communication technologies (ICT) provide means for developing new tools for preventing falls. To enhance adherence to fall prevention interventions, end users need to be engaged from the early phases of the development process. This paper reports the focus group evaluation of five scenarios related to fall risk assessment and fall prevention. There were four focus groups with older adults in both Finland and Spain; 58 participants in all. The most interesting features for the interviewees were usage of intelligent gym equipment, the possibility of peer support and multi-factorial fall risk assessment. The scenario with intelligent gym equipment rose above the others among Finnish participants, while the scenarios were ranked more evenly by Spanish correspondents. The analysis showed that a personal history of falls and a connection to current habits and routines affected the reception of the proposed solutions.

Keywords: fall risk, fall prevention, older adults, ambient assisted living.

1 Introduction

One third of people over the age of 65 fall at least once each year [1]. Falls have a negative effect on a person's quality of life, as they may lead to serious injuries and added fear of falling again, not to mention the increased health care costs [2]. In order to prevent falls efficiently, the fall risk of a person needs to be assessed. As an example, clinically proven assessment scales such as the Berg Balance Scale [3] and Physiological Profile Assessment [4] test postural control and physical functions. Furthermore, the Downton Index [5] also considers previous falls, medication, sensory deficits and mental state to constitute a fall risk index, to mention but a few examples.

According to Gillespie et al. [6], these interventions are likely to be effective, whether targeting multiple risk factors or taking a more specific approach, such as

C. Nugent, A. Coronato, and J. Bravo (Eds.): IWAAL 2013, LNCS 8277, pp. 39–46, 2013.
© Springer International Publishing Switzerland 2013

combined muscle strength and balance training. Optimal approaches involve interdisciplinary collaboration [7]. Individually tailored interventions are found to be especially beneficial in preventing falls [6]. Information and communication technologies (ICT) provide means for developing new tools for fall prevention. In order for interventions to be effective, it is of the utmost importance for the target user to comply with the program. For example, in a fall prevention study in Australia, only 21% of the 5,681 study participants did balance or strength training and just 3% did both following the recommendation of exercising two days a week [8]. Developers must acknowledge the barriers and motivators for physical exercise that older people perceive [9], in order to improve the adherence of such interventions. Thus it is key to engage end users from the earliest stages of the development process.

The aim of our research is to iteratively develop and evaluate tools for fall risk assessment and fall prevention. This paper reports the results from a cross-cultural focus group evaluation of five functional scenarios of the prospective system with older adults in two countries: Finland and Spain.

2   Methods

2.1   Scenarios

The scenarios are narrative stories that explain the functionalities and flow of events of the system from the end-users' point of view. Five different scenarios were jointly created by the research partners, who have backgrounds in fields such as mathematics, economics, medicine and software engineering. Short descriptions of the main features are explained in Table 1.

Table 1. Main Features of the Evaluated Scenarios

Scenario	Users	Main features
A: Fall risk assessment and prescription of fall prevention interventions	Elsa, 80 years old, living at home Doctor, physical therapist, nurse Elsa's daughter	- doctor, physical therapist, Elsa and Elsa's daughter fill in fall risk assessment scales - combined fall risk estimate based on all the scales and tests - guidance for fall prevention based on test results - follow-up
B: Self-monitoring of fall risk	Lisa, 65 years old, living at home	- guidance through home terminal device to perform certain physical tasks while wearing an activity monitor - fall risk calculation - statistics and exercise guidance based on results - data transfer to central database (for doctors etc.)
C: Active fall prevention	Helmi, 82 years old, living at home with her husband and dog Physical therapist	- intelligent equipment at the gym - personal ID card that can be inserted into apparatuses at the gym for viewing of exercise plans and automatic follow-up - data transfer to the home computer with the same ID card

Table 1. (*continued*)

D: ADL monitor & fall prevention system	David, normal healthy person, 65-75 years old General practitioner	- monitoring of activities of daily living (partly automatic, partly self-registered) through home system (PC, webcam, smartphone) - proposing physical and mental exercises based on ADL assessment - alert in case of deterioration trend and prompt for a visit to the general practitioner
E: Fall prevention by building confidence, physical exercise and social support	Aino and Reino, retired couple, 75-80 years old	- intervention club (a group of older adults who want to prevent falls) all provided with a home device (e.g. tablet) - exercise guidance and information videos (motivation, safety, etc.) - monitoring of exercises performed - peer support by other club members via the device: comparison of results, discussions, motivation

2.2   Focus Group Evaluation

Four focus group interviews, with 5-8 older adult participants in each, were organized in Tampere, Finland (N=29 in total, aged 63-93 years, mean 74 years). The recruited voluntary participants were residents of privately owned senior houses. Furthermore, four focus group interviews, with 5-10 older adult participants, were organized in Madrid, Spain (N=29 in total, aged 56-96 years, mean 73 years). Two of the groups were of patients at the Hospital La Fuenfría; a third group's participants were independently living senior citizens, members of the Cultural Centre in the town of Cercedilla (Madrid), and a fourth group were also independently living older people attending the Primary Care Centre of Monterrozas in Las Rozas (Madrid).

After a short introduction to the project, the participants were asked to fill in a background questionnaire about demographics, current usage and attitudes towards technology, fall history and possible conditions affecting their balance. The scenarios were explained one by one, while a picture or a sketch elucidating the story was shown to the participants. After each scenario the interviewees filled in a questionnaire with six aspects adopted from Ikonen et al. [10]: credibility, usefulness, ease of use, adoptability, ethicality and desirability. Each aspect was rated on a five-point Likert scale; strongly agree, agree, undecided, disagree and strongly disagree. In addition, a willingness to pay option was included in the questionnaire for each scenario in the Spanish focus groups, whereas in the Finnish focus groups this topic was covered in the discussion.

The moderators encouraged the participants to freely discuss the scenarios in order to elicit open comments and gather possible improvement ideas. Through semi-structured discussion before and after the scenario evaluation, the participants were asked about their current knowledge of fall risks and perceptions on fall prevention activities. The discussions were recorded for later analysis.

2.3   Data Analysis

To compare the different scenarios a Goodness Grade, applied from Kenttä et al. [11], was calculated for each scenario. The answers for the Likert items were translated into numerical form from -2 to 2, with 2 representing the answer "strongly agree" and

-2 "strongly disagree", respectively. The sum of all the answers for the same question is adjusted for answer frequency to that particular question. The results are presented as percentages from -50 to 50.

The focus group recordings were examined to collect the comments emerging during the scenario evaluation and the semi-structured discussions.

It is also important to note that the Likert items represent individual 'attitude' or 'opinion' with respect to a statement. The statement can be apparently logical, even close to a formal predicate in first-order logic, but the specific Likert item selected should not necessarily be seen as an objective truth value that the individual attaches to the statement. Some responders in a population might have a stronger background for logical thinking, some a weaker one. This means, on the one hand, that responses are not always comparable and, on the other, that transference from Likert items and scales to other items and scales must be done with the utmost care. Furthermore, test groups responding with Likert items are usually not given any detailed guidelines, e.g. concerning the difference between 'agree' and 'strongly agree'.

2.4 Statistical Power

Hypothesis testing is comparing mean values for population groups. If the mean values are closer to being the same, we are closer to the 'truth' concerning the null hypothesis, i.e., closer to 'not significant', which means we have not found enough evidence against the null hypothesis. Conversely, 'significance' means having found evidence against the null hypothesis, i.e., there is a 'significant' difference in the mean values. Note, however, that "no evidence for difference" is not the same as "no difference".

In our paper, the sample size is rather small relative to conventional ways of providing power calculations, which focus on type II error, i.e., false negatives. However, the sample size is not "too small" to provide some discussions and reach some conclusions, e.g. about differences in means.

Suppose we aim at a statistical significance level of 0.05 with 80% power. Then the sample size, using Altman's monograms [12], should be

$$n = \frac{2}{d^2} \times c_{0.05;80\%} \tag{1}$$

in each arm of the trial, where the standardized difference is the ratio between difference in mean and standard deviation

$$d = \frac{(mean_1 - mean_2)}{\sqrt{\frac{(var_1 + var_2)}{2}}}. \tag{2}$$

As an example, consider the sample divided into two fairly equal-sized groups. As $c_{0.05;80\%} = 7.9$ and the groups' answers have a difference in means of close to 0.5 and variances close to 1, according to (1) and (2), we obtain an ideal sample size of n = 63. I.e., we are fairly close the ideal sample size for a typical hypothesis testing. These observations also show how extended tests can be performed.

3   Results

3.1   Questionnaire Results

At least one of the six aspects (credibility, usefulness, ease of use, adoptability, ethicality and desirability) was evaluated by all the focus group participants for scenarios A and B. In addition, some participants did not evaluate all the scenarios resulting in response rates of 87.9%, 89.7%, and 86.2% for scenarios C, D, and E respectively. The first Spanish group with five people was not presented with scenarios C, D and E.

Fig. 1 presents the overall and separate goodness grades for Finland and Spain for each scenario. On a scale from -50 to 50, scenario C scored the highest total goodness grade of 22.6, as it did in both countries separately. In Finland, scenario C was clearly the best received, with a score of 26.8, whereas in Spain the ratings were more even.

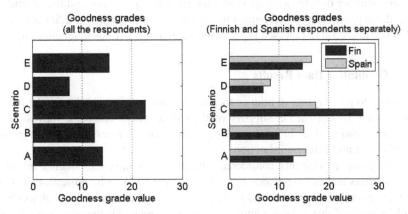

Fig. 1. Left: Goodness grades among all respondents (N=58). Right: Goodness grades among Finnish (N=29) and Spanish (N=29) interviewees separately.

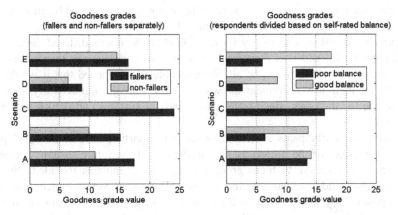

Fig. 2. Left: Goodness grades among subjects based on number of falls during the last year; one or more falls (N=28) and zero falls (N=30). Right: Goodness grades among subjects based on self-rated balance; poor or very poor (N=11) and moderate to very good (N=47).

28 of 58 focus group participants had fallen at least once during the previous year and 64.3% of those still rated their balance as moderate or better, and 32.1% as good or very good. Fig. 2 illustrates how people with a history of falls rated each scenario compared to non-fallers, and how people with poor self-rated balance answered compared to people with good self-rated balance.

There was a clear correlation between the desirability to use an ICT-based fall prevention system and current computer use. Using the average of all answers to the questionnaire, the mean to the question "I would like to use it" among those using a computer is 2.38 while the mean among those not using a computer is 2.97 (5 representing absolute rejection and 1 absolute willingness). The difference in mean is therefore 0.59.

Willingness to pay was introduced separately for each scenario in the Spanish questionnaire. The results correspond with the qualification given to each scenario. The first number denotes average points for all seven questions, and the second number is the average for the willingness to pay question: A 2.5/3.1; B 2.5/3.0; C 2.4/2.6; D 2.7/3.1; E 2.4/3.0 (5 representing absolute rejection and 1 absolute willingness).

3.2   Qualitative Data Results

According to participants in both countries, external factors were by far the most important cause of falling, i.e. slippery roads, bad footwear and rugs. Intrinsic factors that were mentioned included poor muscle strength, dizziness, low blood pressure, fear of falling and cerebral infarction.

Focus group participants considered education important, i.e. sharing information about fall risks and fall prevention either among their peers or by professionals. Finnish interviewees called the topic of fall prevention very well known by them, although some people considered that it doesn't apply to them at this point. On the other hand, the Spanish older adults complained about a lack of structured information about falls before they or people in their near circle fall. In addition to proper footwear and environmental modifications, such as removing rugs, many of the respondents suggested balance exercises and strength training as means for preventing falls.

Opinions on willingness to pay for these kinds of solutions differed. Some considered them useful and said they would pay at least some money themselves while others were not willing to pay at all. Some people were worried that it wouldn't be possible on their low retirement allowance. They said the municipality should be responsible for the costs, since using these kinds of systems can reduce health care expenses.

Many of the participants expressed an interest in participating in the development in the later stages of the project as field trial users of the future system. Scenario C was the most attractive to focus group participants. Comments included: "It is the most feasible" and "most usable in real life". The social aspect of scenario E was found positive by many. They valued the peer support and cooperation features. However, there were some that thought they might feel pressured when it came to comparing their own performance with others.

The usage of the word "computer" in the scenarios caused ambivalence among some users who did not currently own a computer. Some suspected that the proposed solutions could not be implemented in real life. There were worries about who would carry out the fall risk evaluations and how much they would cost.

4   Discussion

The overall goodness of all scenarios was positively evaluated, since there were no negative grades on the scale from -50 to 50. The three best-liked scenarios, those introducing intelligent gym equipment, peer support, and multi-factorial fall risk assessment, were the same in both countries, Finland and Spain. In Finland, scenario C rose clearly above the others. One contributory factor may be that it was the most familiar to many of the Finnish interviewees, since most of them were actively going to gym already. Scenario D, with the lowest goodness grade in both countries, may have been too technical for many and difficult to understand. It contained several different features and perhaps should have been broken down into smaller sub-scenarios. In addition, it should be noted that the personality of the moderator may have had an effect on the results, as participants were divided into subgroups led by different moderators.

Interestingly, people with a history of falls usually gave better ratings to the proposed scenarios than non-fallers. This could indicate that people who have fallen before are, on average, keener on fall prevention. At the same time, people who rated their balance better evaluated all the scenarios better than people with poor self-rated balance. This might arise from the fact that, for people with poor balance, it is difficult to perform the physical activities that are part of most scenarios. Also Stevens et al. [13] reported that older adults often believe themselves to be too old or frail for physical exercise.

The participants were quite well aware of fall risks, which may be due to the fact that they were recruited on a voluntary basis, implying that only people interested in fall prevention participated. Similarly to Stevens et al. [13], the first responses to the question on causes of falls usually related to extrinsic factors rather than intrinsic factors.

There were some interviewees in the focus groups that did not currently own computers, which caused some confusion for them. However, the situation will presumably be different in the future, since older adults ten years from now will most probably be used to working with computers.

In future work, evaluation results will be used for system requirement specifications. Similar focus group interviews will also be organized with professional end users, e.g. physical therapists, doctors and other caregivers. Furthermore, it would be interesting to evaluate the same scenarios at the end of the project to observe possible changes in older adults' perceptions and attitudes towards the presented ideas.

Acknowledgments. This study was conducted under the Ageing in Balance project, which is a part of the European Ambient Assisted Living Joint Program (AAL JP). The authors would like to thank all the focus group participants and especially YH Kodit Oy and Kotosalla foundation in Finland, and Cercedilla Town Hall and Centro de Salud Monterrozas in Spain for their contribution.

References

1. Lord, S.R., Sherrington, C., Menz, H.B.: Falls in older people: Risk factors and strategies for prevention. Cambridge Univ. Press (2001)
2. WHO Global Report on Falls Prevention in Older Age. World Health Organization, France (2007)
3. Berg, K.O., Wood-Dauphinee, S.L., Williams, J.I., Gayton, D.: Measuring balance in elderly: preliminary development of an instrument. Physiotherapy Canada 41, 304–311 (1989)
4. Lord, S.R., Menz, H.B., Tiedemann, A.: A physiological profile approach to falls risk assessment and prevention. Phys. Ther. 83, 237–252 (2003)
5. Downton, J.H.: Falls in the elderly, pp. 128–130. Edward Arnold, London (1993)
6. Gillespie, L.D., Gillespie, W.J., Robertson, M.C., Lamb, S.E., Cumming, R.G., Rowe, B.H.: Interventions for preventing falls in elderly people. Cochrane Database of Systematic Reviews (4) (2003); Re-published online with edits: 21 January 2009 in Issue 1 (2009)
7. Rubenstein, L.Z.: Falls in older people: epidemiology, risk factors and strategies for prevention. Age Ageing 35, 37–41 (2006)
8. Merom, D., Pye, V., Macniven, R., van der Ploeg, H., Milat, A., Sherrington, C., Lord, S., Bauman, A.: Prevalence and correlates of participation in fall prevention exercise/physical activity by older adults. Prev. Med. 55, 613–617 (2012)
9. Schutzer, K.A., Sue Graves, B.: Barriers and motivations to exercise in older adults. Prev. Med. 39, 1056–1061 (2004)
10. Ikonen, V., Niemelä, M., Kaasinen, E.: Scenario-based design of ambient intelligence. In: Proc. 3rd Int. Symp. UCS, Seoul, Korea, pp. 57–72 (2006)
11. Kenttä, O., Merilahti, J., Petäkoski-Hult, T., Ikonen, V., Korhonen, I.: Evaluation of technology-based service scenarios for supporting independent living. In: Proc. 29th Ann. Int. Conf. IEEE EMBS, Lyon, France, pp. 4041–4044 (2007)
12. Altman, D.G.: Practical Statistics for Medical Research. Chapman & Hall (1991)
13. Stevens, J.A., Noonan, R.K., Rubenstein, L.Z.: Older adult fall prevention: perceptions, beliefs, and behaviours. Am. J. Lifestyle Med. 4, 16–20 (2010)

Enhancing Social Interaction between Older Adults and Their Families

Diego Muñoz, Francisco Gutierrez, Sergio F. Ochoa, and Nelson Baloian

Computer Science Department, Universidad de Chile
Av. Blanco Encalada 2120, 3rd Floor, Santiago, Chile
{dimunoz,frgutier,sochoa,nbaloian}@dcc.uchile.cl

Abstract. The rise of Internet and ubiquitous technologies have spread and diversified the social media used by people to interact among them. Unfortunately most older adults are not able to use these solutions. This situation isolates them and negatively affects their physical and mental health. Aiming to improve mood in older adults, and helping them overcome the negative effects of social isolation, we have developed a computer-based intermediary system, that we called Social Connector. This system is capable of boosting the social interaction between an elder and his/her close relatives; e.g. adult children and grandchildren. The system can also be used as a sensor of elders' social interactions and mood. The preliminary evaluation results indicate that the system is well accepted by older adults, and it can be used to boost social interactions with their relatives.

Keywords: Social interaction, social isolation, older adults, ambient intelligence, accessibility.

1   Introduction

Today, social media help people enhance and increase their social interactions. Unfortunately, older adults usually lack the required knowledge and technological background needed to participate in these platforms. Therefore this evolution of social interaction media typically excludes older adults and socially isolates them. As an example, according to the 2012 census data for Chile [4], only a 28.5% of the population over 50 years old is able to search information in the Web, a 25.6% declare to know how to send e-mails, and a 70.5% is not able to perform neither of these tasks. Moreover, according to Internet World Stats [12], the Internet usage penetration in Chile is 59.2%, the second highest one in the region. These values put in evidence a generation gap in terms of technological adoption and usage, since adults over 50 years old in Chile account for a 28.1% of the country population.

While elder people prefer social interactions based on telephone, letters and face-to-face communication, the new generations go towards mobile computing and social networking services. This has caused the emergence of three different generations, according to their preferred social interaction mechanisms: the *digital natives*, who grew up with the Internet-based and mobile technology; the *digital immigrants*, who

C. Nugent, A. Coronato, and J. Bravo (Eds.): IWAAL 2013, LNCS 8277, pp. 47–54, 2013.

positively adopted these technologies; and the *digital illiterate*, who failed in this adoption, or were not affected by the introduction of these technologies. If we consider a typical family, it is quite possible that the older adults are digital illiterate, but their grandchildren are digital natives. Figure 1 depicts the evolution of the social interaction channels of a family community, during the last years, based on the interaction tools preferred by their members.

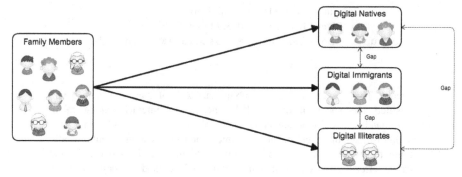

Fig. 1. Social interaction channels evolution

This technological shift pushes older adults to acquire new knowledge. However, elders are limited to address that challenge, due that one of the most common consequences of aging is the impairment of cognitive ability. This translates into a reduction of biological and mental capacities, such as visual and auditory perception, fine motor control and some aspects of memory and cognition [3, 8]. Therefore, these people need support and guidance to face this complex scenario in a pleasant way [15]. Otherwise, the technological adoption by older adults dramatically diminishes.

The social isolation that affects older adults is mostly due to their low capabilities of using technological solutions that were not properly designed for them, such as most social networking services and e-mail applications. This phenomenon leads to harmful effects on their physical and mental health. In fact, social isolation and low stimulation can be linked to changes on hormone production in human beings [2], and more specifically, a reduction on the levels of DHEA, a hormone used for slowing or reversing aging, improving thinking skills in older people, and slowing the progress of Alzheimer's disease [13]. Therefore, it is relevant to identify alternative interaction mechanisms that can be used by older adults, since the social isolation can directly impact on their behavior, physical and emotional sensibility, and interpersonal empathy.

Aiming to improve mood in older adults, and helping them overcome the negative effects of social isolation, we developed a computer-based intermediary system, that we called *Social Connector*. This system is capable of boosting social interaction between older adults and their close relatives. The Social Connector plays two roles: (1) to try to reduce the gap between the social interaction scenarios preferred by the older adults and digital natives, digital immigrants and other digital illiterate; and (2) to act as a mood sensor in people, by triggering warnings and other notification mechanisms to alert and support those in need. The system takes advantage of the sensing devices embedded in computers (particularly in slates) to implement presence awareness mechanisms.

Next section reports the related work. Section 3 presents the architecture of the social connector and its main components. Section 4 shows the implemented prototype and describes the main use scenarios. Section 5 discusses the preliminary results. Section 6 presents the conclusions and further work.

2   Related Work

Cornejo et al. [5] studied how situated displays can provide ambient awareness to strengthen the family social network of older adults. The authors found that these mechanisms can assist the integration of older adults to their social networks, and therefore contribute to enhance asymmetric relations between them and their younger relatives.

Aiming to support intergenerational social interactions, Dianti et al. [6] designed and developed two interconnected applications that provide communication between elders and young people through a common infrastructure. At one side, the application featured a messaging application, developed for smartphones; on the other side, older adults used a tablet-oriented application that worked as a display of all received messages and pictures.

Moser et al. [14] claim that one problem for older adults, is that information systems often do not allow feeling or sensing their communication partners. Therefore, there is a need of designing for enhancing the feeling of belongingness in order to gain social presence.

Kirk et al. [10] showed that home users of video-mediated communication achieve a closer connection with their families and friends. However, most video conferencing systems are designed for phone-calls between only two locations. Therefore, using them for long interactions or social gatherings with multiple families is cumbersome [9]. Ames et al. [1] concluded that older adults enjoy interacting through videoconferencing software, since they could talk with their relatives longer, and get to know them better. In fact, one of the greatest rewards perceived by the elderly was the aspect of "being there".

Kurniawan and Zaphiris [11] proposed a set of guidelines that can help Web designers ensure accessibility and usability of Web pages for older adults. These guidelines include concerns specific to targets, graphics, navigation, browser features, content layout design, links, user cognitive design, use of color and background, text design, search engines, and user feedback and support. Finally, Wu and Van Slyke [16] studied the relationship between functionality and perceived usefulness, and between functionality and perceived ease of use, in the case of senior, casual, and novice users.

3   Architecture of the Social Connector

The Social Connector adheres to a client-server architecture. The server is used mainly to provide persistency to the community setting information and also to the data shared by their members. Two client applications interact with the server: one for elders (that was designed to run on a slate), and a Web system for adults and young people (Fig. 2). Both client applications allow the exchange of public and private messages among community members, and also performing videoconferences using Skype. However, the Web application allows community managers to change the community settings (e.g. to add or remove members, or change users roles). Regular users can modify their own profile (e.g. name or picture) using the Web client (through the Family management module).

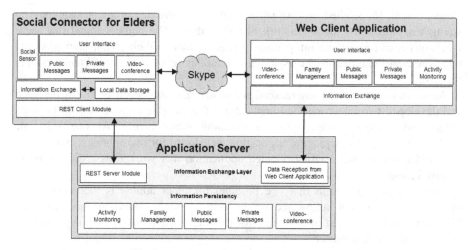

Fig. 2. Architecture of the Social Connector

The Social Connector for elders includes a social sensor that identifies people in the environment where the device is installed. The sensing service is performed through voice analysis in real-time, using the OpenSmile framework [7]. This analysis allows identifying people, their gender and some moods of them. When the social connector module detects sadness, it sends a private message to people monitoring the identified elder, indicating such a situation. This sensing service allows the rest of family members both, to detect temporal or permanent anomalous situations that are not clearly visible for them, and take action to address these situations early.
Both client applications use the *activity monitor* to record the user interactions in a log file, which can be accessed and analyzed by the community managers using the Web client. An information exchange module is used to keep the coherence between the shared information available in both, server and client applications. The server keeps in different repositories information about different components (i.e. social activities, family management, public/private messages and videoconferences).

4   Services for Elders

The user interface of the Social Connector is simple (Fig. 3a), in order to help elders understand it and help themselves feel comfortable with it. The available services allow users to perform videoconferences, and send/receive private or public messages. The slate running the system was installed on a wall (Fig.3b), and it was kept connected at all times to the electrical network and Internet. This avoids that elder people have to be aware of connection issues.

(a)   (b)

Fig. 3. Implementation of the Social Connector

The elders use their voice to communicate with other family members, and use their hands only to select the service to be used. After using a service, the system automatically detects inactivity and presents (by default) the main user interface. This mechanism avoids that elders have to deal with the regular windows used in most software applications.

The videoconference module was implemented using the Skype API. Fig. 4a shows the list of contacts that is visible to the elders. This service allows other family members to call them using the regular Skype system, which typically eases the interaction because the communication tool does not represent an obstacle for them. Usually, the rest of the family prefers to use their regular interaction supporting systems (e.g. email, Skype, Facebook) to communicate with other relatives, instead of using a proprietary system where they have to log in to interact with the others. This aspect of the system, i.e. the usability for adults and young people, was identified as a key design issue during the system evaluation. Therefore it has been partially addressed in the current version of the Social Connector.

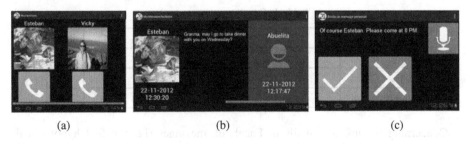

(a)   (b)   (c)

Fig. 4. User interfaces of the Social Connector

Following the same idea, the private messages have been implemented as e-mails, which allow family members to use regular email systems to deliver these messages to elders. A filter embedded in the *private messages* component shows on the interface only the messages of the family members. Fig. 4b shows the user interface in which the elders visualize these messages. Elders respond to private messages using the voice (Fig. 4c). A speech-to-text translator converts the voice message and shows it on the screen. If the user agrees, the message is sent (as a regular e-mail). Otherwise, a new message response can be recorded, or the user can decide to not respond to the message.

5   Preliminary Results

In order to obtain preliminary information about the acceptance of the system, we installed it at the living room of a house where three elderly people live, one male and two females aged 76, 74 and 70 years old respectively. All of them are digital illiterate. They used the system for three days in order to communicate with their sons (digital immigrants, aged 54, 47, 46 and 39 years old) and grandchildren (digital natives, aged 22, 21, 16, 13). Since the goal of this activity was just to have some first impressions about how the users would react to the system, we did not prepare any formal experiment.

After that period, we conducted three focus groups: one for each group (i.e. elders, adults and young people). All of them considered the application usable and useful, however they also indicated some limitations that allow us to understand some social interaction patterns between these groups.

The focus group addressed three hypothetical situations: *Suppose you have to send a message to another person, how often would you do it if:* (1) the message can be sent by e-mail or through a Facebook message (the alternative you prefer); (2) the message can be sent through a Web page in which you must enter a username and password; (3) the message can be sent through a system where you dictate the message to the computer (i.e. you talk to the computer). For each situation, the answer options were: *a. always, b. occasionally,* or *c. rarely or never.* Table 1 presents the answers, indicating for each situation the type of response that was obtained (i.e. options "a", "b" or "c").

Table 1: Results of the survey

	1.a	1.b	1.c	2.a	2.b	2.c	3.a	3.b	3.c
Young	4/4	-	-	-	2/4	2/4	2/4	1/4	1/4
Adults	4/4	-	-	-	1/4	3/4	-	1/4	3/4
Elders	1/4	-	3/4	-	-	-	4/4	-	-

Concerning the use of e-mails or Facebook messages (i.e. the first hypothetical situation), young people and adults feel comfortable with it, but the elders not. Only one elder knew how to send e-mails. Concerning the use of a Web system to interact with others, it was not a good option for young people and particularly for elders. In the case of the adults, they mentioned that they would use it only if the person to be contacted is affectively very close to them (e.g. their parents or children). Concerning the use of voice to support these interactions, it seems to be quite suitable for young people, but mainly for elders. The adults' opinion was similar to the previous situation; i.e. they would use the system if the person to be contacted were very close.

Although these results are still preliminary, they indicate that the three groups would prefer to use different interactions tools, and the adults are the only ones that are willing to use a tool that they consider to not being suitable for them, in the case they have an important emotional tie towards the other. Young people prefer interaction tools that are natural to them, and the elders mentioned that they want simple solutions. One of them mentioned: "*at this point you do not want to complicate your life*". These preliminary results represent an important insight to rethink the design of the interaction paradigms considered in the Social Connector; particularly the support for interactions used by young and adults.

Finally, a last question was done to the participants during the focus group: *Would you like that the system inform you when a family member is depressed or sad?* All of them answered "yes" and would be eager to count on such a service. This means the Social Connector has an interesting chance to act as an emotional sensor of people (particularly elders), and thus enhance the social activity and tie the links among members of a familiar network.

6   Conclusions and Future Work

This article presents a system that was initially designed to help reduce the social isolation experienced by elder people, due to the lack of knowledge to use Internet-based interaction tools. After a first evaluation round, we identified that the system can also be used to monitor elders' mood (through a social sensor), and also support interactions among other family members.

Because of the gap that exists between the interaction tools preferred by young, adults and elder people, the system provides some mechanisms to address it. However, more research and evaluation is required to make a definitive proposal.

The Social Connector was evaluated by elders, adults and young people, all members of a family community. The participants found the system to be usable and useful, and the weaknesses that they identified are related to mitigating the already mentioned gap. In the focus groups conducted after the evaluation process, several participants mentioned that they would like that the system allows them to interact in an ubiquitous way; i.e. that every member uses the system that is more suitable for him/her, which is clearly the next step in this research.

Concerning the *social sensor* included in the solution, all the participants were eager to user the system and were very enthusiastic to count on that service, particularly when monitoring elders that do not have a caregiver. The social interactions carried during the evaluation process did not require the triggering of alarms indicating sadness of any elder; therefore, the social sensor service was not visible for the participants in the process.

Although this is a first step in this research initiative, these preliminary results allow us to expect a positive impact of the Social Connector on the elders' mood, the monitoring capability in these people, and the interactions among family community members.

Acknowledgments. This work has been supported by Fondecyt (Chile), Grant N° 1120207. The work of Francisco Gutierrez has been supported by the Conicyt (Chile) Ph.D. scholarship.

References

1. Ames, M.G., Go, J., Kaye, J., Spasojevic, M.: Making Love in the Network Closet: The Benefits and Work of Family Videochat. In: Proc. of CSCW 2010, Savannah, USA (2010)
2. Arnetz, B., Theorell, T., Levi, L., Kallner, A., Eneroth, P.: An Experimental Study of Social Isolation of Elderly People: Psychoendocrine and Metabollic Effects. Psychosomatic Medicine 45(4), 395–406 (1983)
3. Carmichael, A.: Style Guide for the Design of Interactive Television Services for Elderly Viewers, Independent Television Commission, Winchester, United Kingdom (1999)
4. Chile 2012 Census, http://www.censo.cl (last visit: September 15, 2013)
5. Cornejo, R., Tentori, M., Favela, J.: Ambient Awareness to Strengthen the Family Social Network of Older Adults. Computer Supported Cooperative Work 22, 309–344 (2013)
6. Dianti, M., Parra, C., Casati, F., De Angelli, A.: What's Up: Fostering Intergenerational Social Interactions. In: Proc. of the FoSIBLE 2012, Marseille, France (2012)
7. Eyben, F., Weninger, F., Woellmer, M., Schuller, B.: OpenSMILE: The Munich Versatile and Fast Open-Source Audio Feature Extractor, http://opensmile.sourceforge.net (last visit: September 15, 2013)
8. Hawthorn, D.: Possible Implications of Aging for Interface Designers. Interacting with Computers 12, 151–156 (2000)
9. Judge, T.K., Neustaedter, C., Harrison, S., Blose, A.: Family Portals: Connecting Families Through a Multifamily Media Space. In: Proc. CHI 2011, Vancouver, Canada (2011)
10. Kirk, D., Sellen, A., Cao, X.: Home Video Communication: Mediating 'Closeness'. In: Proc. of CSCW 2010, Savannah, United States (2010)
11. Kurniawan, S., Zaphiris, P.: Research-Derived Web Design Guidelines for Older People. In: Proc. ASSETS 2005, Baltimore, USA (2005)
12. Latin American Internet and Facebook Population – Telecommunications Statistics, http://www.internetworldstats.com/stats10.htm (last visited: September 15, 2013)
13. MedlinePlus, http://www.nlm.nih.gov/medlineplus/druginfo/natural/331.html (last visit: September 15, 2013)
14. Moser, C., Fuchsberger, V., Neureiter, K., Sellner, W., Tscheligi, M.: Elderly's Social Presence supported by ICTs – Investigating User Requirements for Social Presence. In: Proc. of SocialCom 2011, Boston, USA (2011)
15. Roupa, Z., Nikas, M., Gerasimou, E., Zafeiri, V., Giasyrani, L., Kazitori, E., Sotiropoulou, P.: The Use of Technology by the Elderly. Health Science J. 4(2), 118–126 (2010)
16. Wu, Y., Van Slyke, C.: Interface Complexity and Elderly Users: Revisited. In: Proc. of the SAIS 2005, Savannah, United States (2005)

Personalization of Serious Videogames
for Occupational Engagement for Elderly

Mario A. Bruno[1], Roberto G. Aldunate[2], and Jaime Meléndez[3]

[1] DCI-Facultad de Ingeniería/Advanced Research Center,
Universidad de Playa Ancha, Valparaíso, Chile
mbruno@upla.cl
[2] University of Illinois at Urbana-Champaign, Illinois, USA
aldunate@illinois.edu
[3] Escuela de Psicología, Universidad de Valparaíso, Valparaíso, Chile
jaime.melendez@uv.cl

Abstract. Recently, the use of video games has been extended to attenuate the cognitive deterioration in elderly. However, not all interventions based on videogames have shown benefits, and very limited research has been made on the design and evaluation of serious videogames that promote a change of attitude in the players, along with entertainment, to properly develop cognitive skills. To this end we have developed a serious videogame prototype to support occupational engagement, based on personalization, that incorporates strategies to encourage and reward with a more meaningful and well-defined purpose for the elderly, and validated it by an expert in cognitive psychology. As a result, although it is needed to adjust levels of competitiveness and provide a positive reward to player achievements, such videogame can support elderly behaviors to social participation that is considered a relevant issue in Chilean society, as it raises challenging issues for cognitive stimulation.

Keywords: Serious videogames, elderly, occupational engagement, cognitive performance.

1   Introduction

Technological advances offer many possibilities to stimulate cognitive performance, which in turn could lead to improving the quality of life of people, especially the elderly and those pre-retirement. All physical deterioration of the body due to aging (including the central nervous system [1]) can mean cognitive decay, which should not be confused with that caused by neurodegenerative disease of Alzheimer type. In fact, most of the elderly population shows no neurodegenerative disorders such as cognitive or affective disorders [2], which prevent normal adaptation to society. They can be cognitively capable of many skills, especially if they are constantly stimulated and follow an appropriate relationship with the social context.

Recent studies in [3-4], have shown that the use of videogames attenuates overall cognitive decline in the elderly. However, not all interventions based on videogames

C. Nugent, A. Coronato, and J. Bravo (Eds.): IWAAL 2013, LNCS 8277, pp. 55–62, 2013.
© Springer International Publishing Switzerland 2013

have shown benefits. Currently, serious videogames have been developed in the fields of education and health, among others. A serious videogame is not meant to be played for mere entertainment, but as a context with rules among adversaries trying to accomplish an explicit and carefully planned educational purpose [5]. A further approaching requires testing the adaptability which is informed by the player [6] to such videogames, under a methodology to develop strategies that enhance self-regulation, self-care and boost of cognitive functions, expressed in terms of improving the behavioral capacity of elderly to improve the quality of life and autonomy. To illustrate the difference, consider some actions to be performed on the popular video game Halo that are described in Fig. 1. This figure shows a behavior tree diagram. For grasping the notation the reader can see Section 4.1.

In this scenario, when the *Combat* sequence node is evaluated it executes all its child nodes {*Melee*, *Shoot*, *Approach*} from left to right, and the logical conjunction of their success conditions is checked in order to return success. Since such sequence of actions is mostly oriented to decision-making for entertainment, it does not represent a strategy to promote and reward something more meaningful, with a well-defined purpose associated with learning as well as strategies that support elderly to develop their cognitive skills intentionally. In this paper we propose a serious videogame to support the occupational engagement of elderly. The videogame is modeled using behavior trees that support adaptive behavior. We validate that the prototype encourages elderly cognitive development and prevent psychosocial risk factors.

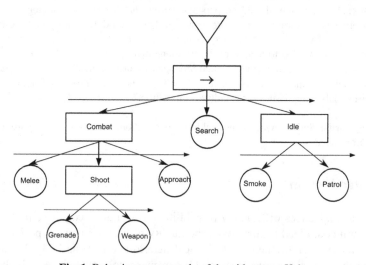

Fig. 1. Behavior tree example of the videogame Halo

2   Cognitive Intervention

The cognitive intervention mainly consists of a group of routines, in which elderly perform working memory and social development tasks which lasts as long as the duration of the intervention. At this point, the serious videogame can deliver positive responses toward the elderly during interventions to promote adherence, through praise, competition, and rewards. In this regard, it is necessary to find some purposeful activity that the elderly user may perform or want to perform. Having ingenious activities, a wide variety of attractive ideas, difficulty adjustment and balance, clear instructions and easy to use commands, so that to enable elderly to gradually overcome obstacles, especially those having to do with presbyopia and some visuospatial difficulties (hand-eye coordination), may prove to be effective for elderly that live a healthy aging. It also involves breaking a "technophobia" barrier.

According to activity theory, elderly must continue to behave as middle-aged people most of the time, keeping all possible activities and replacing lost roles [7]. The promotion of occupational engagement in elderly allows them to address the psychosocial and cognitive decline due to retirement and frailty with advancing age by decreasing stimulation [7]. Occupation permits to maintain wellness, that is, the person's attention develops creativity and activities that promote healthy living styles and social involvement, as well as enhancement of quality of life, through participation in occupation. Occupational performance also provides values, goals and challenges. In addition, cognitive skills are operations and procedures for the acquisition, retention and retrieval of information -that is, memory - that allow elderly to carry out activities, in addition to pass and socialize them (language, motivation and empathy, among others). Cognitive skills are boosted in order to analyze and understand the received information, how it is processed and structured in memory. From the cognitive perspective, learning is conceived as a set of processes that are aimed at information processing. We have then a whole process that starts from the perception of a situation, which activates thinking capacity for decision-making and, finally, performing activities adaptively, creatively and for the individual's social adaptation.

3   Personalization of Serious Videogame to Support Cognitive Performance

A serious videogame can be considered as a mental test to drive a change in attitude among its players, along with the entertainment, according to specific rules to make decisions such as government or corporate training. Serious videogames as such began to be applied in training, for example, in combat simulations for military training. Subsequently, serious video games have been designed for education and health, among others. The adaptability and customization enables that the behavior of serious videogames is sufficiently challenging, difficulty levels are balanced, and scenarios are most likely to be of interest to the player [8]. In order to adjust interventions to the cognitive limitations, it is possible to assess elderly progress to enable them to advance through the levels of difficulty. In this regard, the contents for the audiovisual stimulation should be personalized, by evaluating the parameters and semantic information that carry out the cognitive stimulation (For example, to indicate to the videogame on the obstacles that may be used with the player in decision making), or whether they are related to events produced by the interaction with the user, i.e., the ability of a videogame to provide automated balance ("off-line") or to adjust to its players as they play ("on-line"), concurrently [9].

The behavior of videogames is generally represented using finite state machines FSM, in terms of inputs and outputs that occur at the character, and change the current state, of the videogame. That is, world events can force a change in the state. A FSM describes the produced output events depending on the state of the FSM (i.e., Moore model) or inputs of state and machine (i.e., Mealy model). FSM can be represented by state transition diagrams and "if-then-else" scripts, among others. To represent non-player characters (NPC), videogames also use techniques of planning and problem solving (case-based reasoning), neural networks, decision trees and genetic algorithms. Some approaches describe the character's behavior and dialogue from system log file that maintain the trace of user interaction [10]. Recently, behavior trees have been used in videogames to organize the behavior, and broadly show its complexity and the essential points that the video game design needs to focus.

4   Case Study: Real Time Strategy Serious Videogame

For our case study we have developed a prototype of a Real-time strategy (RTS) serious videogame using Game Maker Studio®, to stimulate cognitive skills of elderly in the social environment of the hills of Valparaíso city. RTS videogames are mainly based on the player's ability to make decisions, rather than in her/his ability to manipulate controls. RTS video games [11] propose the player micro and macro issues management, spatial and temporal reasoning, decision making under uncertainty, and planning and generation of real-time strategies in the presence of adversaries, where multiple players (people or machines) typically compete for resources and make decisions in 2D worlds. The case study focuses on skills of attention, such as exploration, fragmentation, selection and contra distracting, as well as storing/recovery

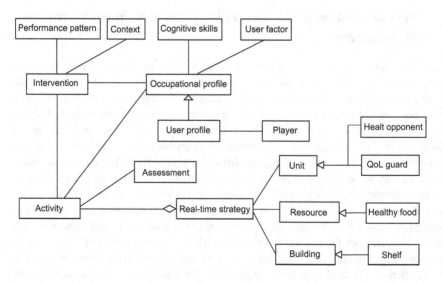

Fig. 2. Domain Model of RTS serious videogame to support occupational engagement

(study techniques or skills), such as coding and generating responses, and semantic networks. A basic example of the latter is read, recite and review 3R. A scenario of the videogame is: "*You go for a walk around the amphitheater of the Valparaiso hills to seek resources to maintain a good quality of life, build foundations for a center of wisdom and face the obstacles.*

The first level is that you get healthy food for lunch today. You find a store on the hill. With the help of quality of life guards you search in the warehouse for ingredients for dinner. You compete with health opponents that are in conflict with healthy food. If you choose an unhealthy ingredient you lose a life. If you gather all the ingredients you build the first base of the center of wisdom, otherwise you must play again".

As described in Fig. 2, activities are performed by elderly in interventions which are based on the outcomes of the assessment process. External or internal contexts to the elderly influence performance patterns, which develop over time and are adopted to perform occupations or activities. User factors such as leisure, work, participation in social or community activities, family, or friends, are related to the occupational profile, which, in turn, is extended by the user profile of the player. Playing the serious videogame permits to boosting cognitive skills, such as attention, understanding, and storage, recovery and processing of information. Formal elements of the RTS videogame include resources, buildings, resource gatherer units and opponent units.

4.1   Behavior Tree

Fig. 3 graphically depicts a behavior tree diagram. The nodes of the tree, except the root node, correspond to tasks, which are organized in a directed acyclic graph, DAG. The leaf nodes (terminal tasks) correspond to action and condition nodes. An action node is represented as a circle, and a condition node is represented as a pentagon. The composite tasks correspond to sequencer and selector nodes. A sequencer node is represented as an arrow inside a rectangle, and a selector node is represented as a question mark inside a rounded rectangle. For composite tasks there are also random and parallel extensions, for modeling non-determinism and concurrency behaviors, respectively. A decorator node is represented as a diamond.

A behavior tree BT can be formally defined as BT = {*Root, S, L, A, C, D*}, where *Root* is the root node, S is a set of sequencer nodes, *L* is a set of selector nodes, *A* is a set of terminal nodes of actions, *C* is a set of conditional terminal nodes, and *D* is a set of decorator nodes. The root node can have only one child node. The sequencer node sequentially executes all of its child nodes, succeeding if all of them are successful. The selector node tests each of its child nodes at a time until one succeeds. The action node changes the state of the world of the videogame. The condition node tests some property of the world of the videogame. The decorator node wraps a single task or child node to improve its behavior. Each node returns either success or failure. Starting from the root, the tree is traversed depth-first, generating a vertical hierarchical structure and decomposition of tasks.

We model behavior of units that help the user using behavior trees. The main characters of the videogame story are the player himself, QoL (Quality of Life) guards and health opponents. Fig. 3 shows the decision making and executable behavior of a QoL guard represented by a behavior tree. In particular in a scenario when the QoL guard cannot see a health opponent. In this case, the guard will gather healthy food if her/his health level is high enough. We start from the root. Then, when the selector has been executed, the first child to be evaluated is the condition NotInOpponentRange?, which returns true if the guard cannot see an opponent, false otherwise. In the case where her health level is not high enough, she/he remains incrementing health.

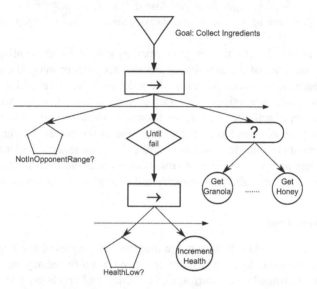

Fig. 3. Behavior tree representing a videogame scenario

The prototype provides, apart from entertainment, several scenarios to measure working memory and episodic memory skills (Fig. 4). Working memory is the process to store and manage information in a short period of time. Episodic memory relates to personal experiences in a given context and moment of time. The videogame can generate positive responses to user progress, also supporting elderly psychological integrity, which allows her/him to be able to self-regulate historic breakthrough on mitigating the decline of cognitive skills. The instructional model consists of providing a tutorial, inviting the user to play again, displaying statistics, and allowing user to view, compete and chat with other players online.

4.2   Validation by the Expert

In the opinion of the expert in Cognitive Psychology and Neuropsychology, the prototype is rather complicated and must have more graduated levels. Moreover, the expert anticipates that the system will be difficult to use by the target audience, as the first level is quite competitive, and fast, therefore, for an elderly would be quite difficult to adapt. If improvements are made regarding larger size instructions, simpler commands, graduated levels, as well as providing permanent feedback in terms of performance as elderly interact with the videogame, i.e., there is a positive reward to the achievements of the player, the videogame would be more effective.

The expert estimates that the developed tool provides a great benefit to the development and maintenance of cognitive skills of the elderly, which is as a relevant issue in Chilean society, in order to support the behaviors for social participation, as poses challenges to the elderly or pre-retirement. Finally, the expert points out that the most valuable feature would be that the serious video game being multiplatform, to suit the conditions of the various institutions working in therapy activities for the elderly.

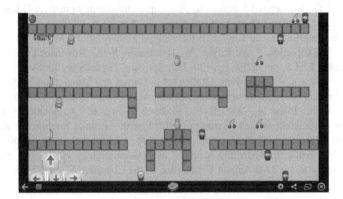

Fig. 4. A first version of the prototype

5   Conclusions

The results from the validation showed that interventions would benefit from serious videogames tailored to the needs of elderly and pre-retirement users. According to the expert a serious videogame may permit, under a multidimensional approach of intervention, to evaluate the development of skills on working and episodic memories so that, by using it systematically, elderly achieve the maintenance of their cognitive skills over a longer period than those not involved in this type of intervention. Although mainly concerned about perceived problems of videogames, the results generate valuable insights on the great potential to support the promotion of healthy lifestyles of people, towards better living conditions and reducing risk factors.

As future work, an improved version of the prototype will be tested in the workshops of the Office of Elderly of the City of Valparaiso, and the Workshop on Social and Cognitive Stimulation in the School of Psychology at the University of Valparaiso.

References

1. Yankner, B.A., Lu, T., Loerch, P.: The Aging Brain. Annu. Rev. Pathol. 3, 41–66 (2008)
2. Diaz, B.E., Martinez Lozano, A.J., Núñez Rodríguez, V.: Características biopsicosociales en una población anciana. Rev. Cubana Enfermer. 19 (2003)

3. Basak, C., Boot, W.R., Voss, M.W., Kramer, A.F.: Can training in a real-time strategy video game attenuate cognitive decline in older adults? Psychology and Aging 23, 765–777 (2008)
4. Stern, Y., Blumen, H.M., Rich, L.W., Richards, A., Herzberg, G., Gopher, D.: Space Fortress game training and executive control in older adults: A pilot intervention. Aging, Neuropsychology, and Cognition 18, 653–677 (2011)
5. Abt, C.C.: Serious Games, pp. 10–14. University Press of America, Lanham (1987)
6. Bakkes, S., Tan, C.T., Pisan, Y.: Personalised gaming: a motivation and overview of literature. In: 8th Australasian Conference on Interactive Entertainment: Playing the System, p. 4. ACM (2012)
7. Kielhofner, G.: Conceptual foundations of occupational therapy practice. G-Reference, Information and Interdisciplinary Subjects Series. FA Davis Co. (2009)
8. Zwartkruis-Pelgrim, E., de Ruyter, B.: Developing an Adaptive Memory Game for Seniors. In: Markopoulos, P., de Ruyter, B., IJsselsteijn, W.A., Rowland, D. (eds.) Fun and Games 2008. LNCS, vol. 5294, pp. 170–181. Springer, Heidelberg (2008)
9. Lopes, R., Bidarra, R.: Adaptivity Challenges in Games and Simulations: A Survey. IEEE Transactions on Computational Intelligence and AI in Games 3, 85–99 (2011)
10. Cheong, Y.-G., Jhala, A., Bae, B.-C., Michael Young, R.: Automatically Generating Summary Visualizations from Game Logs. In: Fourth Artificial Intelligence and Interactive Digital Entertainment Conference, AIIDE 2008. AAAI, Menlo Park (2008)
11. Lewis, J.M., Trinh, P., Kirsh, D.: A corpus analysis of strategy video game play in Starcraft: Brood war. In: 33rd Annual Conference of the Cognitive Science Society, pp. 687–692 (2011)

Return to Activities of Daily Life: Physiotherapy Rehabilitation with Serious Game

Juan Manuel González-Calleros[1], Sergio Arturo Arzola-Herrera[1],
Josefina Guerrero-García[1], Etelvina Archundia-Sierra[1], and Jaime Muñoz-Arteaga[2]

[1] Benemérita Universidad Autónoma de Puebla, Computer Science Faculty, Puebla, Mexico
Av. San Claudio y 14 sur – C.P. 75740 Puebla (México)
juan.gonzalez@cs.buap.mx
http://www.cs.buap.mx/~juan.gonzalez/
[2] Universidad Autónoma de Aguascalientes, Aguascalientes, Mexico
Av. Universidad # 940 – C.P. 20100 Aguascalientes (México)

Abstract. Everyday people suffer from accidents at their home while doing activities of daily life. This results in physical and cognitive injuries that need physiotherapy rehabilitation. Some physiotherapy problems reported by physiotherapists are: lack of patient commitment, lack of motivation and lack of patient feedback to communicate their progress. Thus, it is very frequent that patients abandon their therapy. In this work we investigate the process of creating serious games as a solution to the aforementioned problems. We explore in deep the process of physiotherapy rehabilitation to generate a list of problems and propose a list of requirements as a solution. We present the design using a formal framework to define the analysis, design and some elements of the developed system, which still is in a prototype phase.

Keywords: Rehabilitation, User Interface, Physiotherapy, Serious Game.

1   Introduction

In recent years, technological advancement has allowed the creation of systems which solves problems in different areas, such as business, entertainment as well as the health sector. With the technology advances, health systems for recovery may be easily available to patients at home. They will only need a device where the system can run. Specialists can monitor progress of patients, allowing patients to make their rehabilitation at the time that they can. Although today the advancement of technology is fast, it is always necessary to support people who are not familiar with it, by creating constraints, adjusting them and eliminating them when they are no longer necessary. In this paper we focus on the design aspects of serious games for physiotherapy rehabilitation. Serious games as a mean to provide immersive experiences relevant to the underlying task combined with elements of game-play for education, health and training purposes [8].

Designing and implementing serious games present many technical challenges, and the design of such environments is further more complicated by the rapidly changing

C. Nugent, A. Coronato, and J. Bravo (Eds.): IWAAL 2013, LNCS 8277, pp. 63–66, 2013.
© Springer International Publishing Switzerland 2013

nature of the technology [5]. Serious games have been used in many research projects to provide a motivational context for medical and rehabilitation purposes. Although they have similarities with entertaining games, they must accomplish the objective of the serious game: to educate, to rehabilitate and to confront fears. Research and design of games is a novel area where there is a lot of work to do [1]: design and engineering process to produce fun, evaluation, rapid prototyping, user-centered approaches, and 3DUIs. Designing a patient centred game has been reported in [5,4,7,2] to be closer to the patient's satisfaction. Developing a patient-centred solution still is challenging in the current context using natural user interfaces.

We propose a patient-centered model-driven approach to design the game interaction. We argue that developing serious games is an activity that would benefit from a development method composed of: (1) a set of models defined according to an ontology, (2) a language that expresses these models, and (3) a principle-based approach manipulating these models based on principles. Principles including guidelines and design knowledge helping in the task of creating 3DUIs more close to 3D than 2D.

2   Virtual Spaces for Rehabilitation of Activities of Daily Life

In this section we present the analysis and the design of a serious game with the aim of physiotherapy rehabilitation. The interest is centered in accidents occurred at home that frozen activities of daily life. In particular we will focus our attention to the bathroom since knowledge is just useful within a particular context. We also include the current development of the system which corresponds to a prototype stage.

Requirements elicitation was based on three methods, existing solutions literature review (reported in the state of the art), Participant observation and Interviewing. We visited the physiotherapy clinic of the School of Medicine of the University of Puebla for the participant observation. We saw how therapy is done, the context of therapy and the population. After it, we interviewed physiotherapists, professionals, last year students, and patients to determine their needs, we found that therapy is not just about rehabilitating muscular functions that were damaged by the accident, but it might need to eliminate the fear cause by the accident, for instance, patients reluctant to use the bathroom after the accident. Finally, another aspect to consider is a cognitive problem derived by the accident; memory lost being the most common in the clinic.

One of the problems identified during the observation and confirmed by the interviews, is the lack of motivation and, as a consequence, abandon of the therapy. Different reasons produce this phenomenon: lack of feedback after a session, patients did not know their progress; boring activities and absence of challenge during the therapy; and lack of distractors for pain. Based in these non-functional requirements, we found our solution as good option to solve the aforementioned limitations of current rehabilitation.

The first task is to do the diagnosis of the patient. This is made by using the Kinect camera. The process: an animation shows the patient the movements to do, then the system through acknowledgement of the movement(s) the system determines whether it was right or not. The second task is to determine the required training; this is determined by the physiotherapy expert. The idea is to set objectives and make tests. If the patient fails a test, then a routine (game) which exercises that part of the body is set, this routine should be customized and the doctor should determine the number of repetitions.

Fig. 1. Rehabilitation exercises, from the left side the game of bubble buster, in the right side the game of shaving

From the game's point view, it is considered for each game the successful and fails conditions. We will use the shaving game to illustrate this process (Figure 1). In this case the successful condition is if the face is free of facial hair and the fail condition is if the face is full of hair. The game shows, constant appearance of shaving cream. Then the patient has to shave that particular area in order to get rid of all hair. The system needs to make close up to the user's face in order to be more challenging. It is also possible to define the time for shaving. The objective is to keep the face clean for more time. At the end you receive a message of motivation depending in the results and difficulty. The evolution of this movements and achievements need to be stored in order to see progress. The current development of the system corresponds to a prototype and there is more work ahead. The bottom line is to implement all of mini games. Also to validate routines of rehabilitation with the mini games available.

3   Conclusions

In this paper we introduce a serious game approach for physiotherapy rehabilitation as a solution to the lack of motivation to stay on track with theirs rehabilitation. Furthermore, it makes the task fun distracting them from the pain while it solves other kind of problems like feedback and progression. In the presented work we presented a 2D serious game for rehabilitation of home's accidents, however it is required to a 3D environment in order to project patients more real scenarios. The future work of this research is to create this environment as well as to perform more evaluations related to the benefits of the use of this system. We also need to test the system with real patients and evaluate the system for improvement. There is also more work ahead in terms of the serious game design as discussed before. Regardless of gameplay, the system is different to a traditional therapy because of the following aspects: Challenge, the game is challenging; effort recognition, patients are recognized by the system after doing progressions; sharing and cooperation, patients through the system can share their experiences; imagination, the user interface system can project images to help patients to play in different scenarios. We include in the design some game elements to promote target behaviors and make the game entertaining. Which are:

- Ordered Recognition board. - To appreciate patients' effort into different categories. That is to say, that every achievement would me recorded and presented in the recognition board, however it would be ordered according to the best effort.
- Emoticons. - This will be earned when patients are more confident in the bathroom making explorations and performing tasks quickly and efficient.
- Points. - This evaluates range of motion and progression of patients. The more progression patients get, the more points they get. The more points they get, the higher they will be in the recognition leaderboard.
- Stars. – Patients can give start to others as a gratefulness of help and support. A patient can gives only one star per patient for day, but can gives a star to any amount of patients.
- Final Trophy Badge. - This will be awarded when the patient has successfully recovered from the accident.

Acknowledgements. Mexican PROMEP projects under reference 103.5/12/8136 and 103.5/12/4367.

References

1. Aldrich, C.: The Complete Guide to Simulations and Serious Games: How the Most Valuable Content Will be Created in the Age Beyond Gutenberg to Google. Pfeiffer (2009)
2. Andika, B., Tantra, J., Wai, A.: Interactive Rehabilitation Game Development Using Natural User Interface Devices
3. Calvary, G., Coutaz, J., Thevenin, D., Limbourg, Q., Bouillon, L., Vanderdonckt, J.: A Unifying Reference Framework for Multi-Target User Interfaces. Interacting with Computers 15(3), 289–308 (2003)
4. Feys, P., Alders, G., Gijbels, D., De Boeck, J., De Weyer, T., Coninx, K., Raymaekers, C., Truyens, V., Groenen, P., Meijer, K., Savelberg, H., Op't Eijnde, B.: Arm training in multiple sclerosis using phantom: clinical relevance of robotic outcome measures. In: Proceedings of IEEE 11th International Conference on Rehabilitation Robotics (ICORR 2009), June 23-26, pp. 576–581 (2009)
5. Raymaekers, C., Coninx, K., Gonzalez-Calleros, J.M.: Proceedings of the Design and Engineering of Game-Like Virtual and Multimodal Environment (Deng-VE) Workshop of the ACM SIGCHI Symposium on Engineering Interactive Computing Systems (EICS 2010), June 20 (2010)
6. Vanderdonckt, J.: Model-Driven Engineering of User Interfaces: Promises, Successes, and Failures. In: Buraga, S., Juvina, I. (eds.) Proc. of 5th Annual Romanian Conf. on Human-Computer Interaction (ROCHI 2008), Iasi, Romania, September 18-19, pp. 1–10. Matrix ROM, Bucarest (2008) ISSN 1843-4460
7. Vanacken, L., Notelaers, S., Raymaekers, C., Coninx, K., van den Hoogen, W., IJsselsteijn, W., Feys, P.: Game-based collaborative training for arm rehabilitation of ms patients: A proof-of-concept game. In: Proceedings of GameDays 2009, March 25-26, pp. 65–75 (2009)
8. Zyda, M.: From visual simulation to virtual reality to games. Computer 38(9), 25–32 (2005)

Image Analysis for Crack Detection
in Bone Cement

Carlos Briceño, Jorge Rivera-Rovelo, and Narciso Acuña

Universidad Anahuac Mayab
krlozgod@gmail.com, {jorge.rivera,narciso.acuna}@anahuac.mx

Abstract. This work deals with crack detection in images of bone cements and the method can be applied to other materials. Crack detection and measures obtained from images are useful to characterize the materials, and how the crack evolves according to the effort the material is subject to. This allows to make changes in the composition of the material in order to make it more resistant. The method presented consists of several stages: noise reduction, shadow elimination, image segmentation and path detection for crack analysis. At the end of the analysis of one image, the number of cracks and the length of each one can be obtained. If a video is analyzed, the evolution of cracks in the material can be observed.

1 Introduction

Crack detection and tracking of its growth in materials like bone cement, gives useful information about early stages in fatigue damage; this kind of damage is similar to the one the bones suffer in daily activities. Such information can be used to develop better materials (ie. more resistant materials). Prosthetic bone cement can be used in orthopedics and odontology; it is an acrylic resin used to fix the prosthesis to the bone [1]. This kind of cement is used in orthopedics for hip, knee or shoulder surgery (for example, to replace by a prosthesis), as well as in spinal surgery and dental prosthesis. In such surgery, the bone cement is used to fill the spaces or holes between the (metal) prosthesis and the bone cavity where it should be fixed. According to the norm ASTM E206 described in [2], fatigue is an structural and progressive change, located and persistent, which occurs in materials subject to efforts and fluctuating deformations, which can produce micro-cracks or even total rupture of the material after a sufficiently large number of fluctuations. Fatigue can also be described as a progressive fail which occurs due to crack propagation until they reach an unstable size. For this reason, we should put attention to the materials used in the bone cement and also to its applications, particularly if it implies repeated and fluctuating forces. Fatigue causes failures because of the simultaneous action of cyclic and strain (tension) stress, as well as plastic deformation. The goal of the analysis of the growth of (micro) cracks, is to understand the mechanisms of the beginning and growing of cracks governing early stages of serious damage in bone cement, which are manufactured with monomers of amino group in a matrix of methyl

C. Nugent, A. Coronato, and J. Bravo (Eds.): IWAAL 2013, LNCS 8277, pp. 67–70, 2013.
© Springer International Publishing Switzerland 2013

metacrylate. In this work we deal with the early detection of micro cracks on the surface of bone cement, while they are under fatigue tests, in order to characterize the material and design better and more resistant materials.

2 Method

There are several approaches for crack detection: in [3,4] probabilistic and stochastic theory is applied; [5] uses continuous models, while [6] presents the use of deterministic Markov processes. However all of them deal only with crack detection and does not analyze the growth of the crack, which needs to follow the crack paths during time. The method presented in this paper allows the analysis of crack growing or crack evolution due to its ability to get not only the crack clusters, but also the number and lengths of them. The length of cracks is determined following a *minimum cost path* approach. Figure 1 shows the general scheme of the method. A low pass frequency filter is used for noise

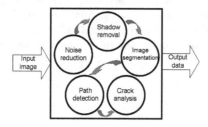

Fig. 1. General scheme of the method

reduction/elimination (Gaussian low pass filter), together with a median filter for elimination of salt and pepper noise (if it is present). Once the noise on the image has been reduced, it could be applied a method for reducing some effect of shadows on the boundaries of the images. Shadows can result in erroneous detection of cracks on the boundaries of the image. To eliminate shadows, a histogram smoothed by a Gaussian kernel with bandwidth B can be used to calculate a threshold, and pixels with gray values over the thresholds are changed for such value. After the stage of preprocessing the image, we need to classify the image pixel into regions (imagge segmentation). Given a pixel, we can determine if it belongs to a segment or to other one by comparing its gray value with a threshold. The threshold value is calculated in such a way that the resulting value can minimize the variance of every segment, and at the same time maximize the variance between segments [7]. That is, we compute the ratio between the two variances and choose as the threshold the value which maximizes that ratio. The weighted within-class variance is given by Eq. (1), where the the class variances are given by Eq. (2), the class probabilities are given by Eq. (3) and the means are given by Eq. (4). $P(i)$ is the probability of the gray value i.

$$\sigma_w^2(t) = q_1(t)\sigma_1^2(t) + q_2(t)\sigma_2^2(t) \tag{1}$$

$$\sigma_1^2(t) = \sum_{i=1}^{t} [i - \mu_1(t)]^2 \frac{P(i)}{q_1(t)} \qquad \sigma_2^2(t) = \sum_{i=t+1}^{I} [i - \mu_2(t)]^2 \frac{P(i)}{q_2(t)} \qquad (2)$$

$$q_1(t) = \sum_{i=1}^{t} P(i) \qquad q_1(t) = \sum_{i=t+1}^{I} P(i) \qquad (3)$$

$$\mu_1(t) = \sum_{i=1}^{t} \frac{iP(i)}{q_1(t)} \qquad \mu_2(t) = \sum_{i=t+1}^{I} \frac{iP(i)}{q_2(t)} \qquad (4)$$

Once we have the segmentation, the crack clusters are detected as neighbor pixels with values under certain threshold; such pixels are considered as vertex of a directed graph. The adjacency of two vertex in the graph is determined with the adjacency of the image pixels: if they are horizontal or vertical neighbors, they are connected with an arrow of length 1; if they are diagonal neighbors, they are connected with an arrow of length $sqrt(2)$. Then, the arrow lengths are modified adding a factor equal to the difference in gray values of the adjacent vertex (connected pixels). Finally, a method to find minimum length paths is used in order to build the paths in each crack cluster (considering that the cracks are associated with the darkest gray values of the pixels).

3 Experimental Results

Figure 2 shows the results with different bandwidth for the Gaussian filter. According to our experiments, the best value for the bandwidth of the Gaussian kernel used is $B = 35$, because in average it produces a threshold which allows a better identification of the cracks in the images. Figure 3 shows the detection of cracks in cement steel subject to strain efforts; the method is applied to the set of images taken from the video of the microscope, and we can track the evolution of the cracks (around 300 frames were processed and we show 4 frames for ilustration).

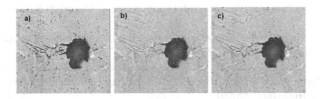

Fig. 2. Results obtained using different bandwidth for the Gaussian kernel used in filtering. Bandwidth: a) 30, b) 35, c) 40.

Fig. 3. Evolution of micro cracks detected in cemented steel images

4 Conclusion

The method described can detect micro cracks in images of materials like bone cement under fatigue efforts. To accomplish such task several steps are needed, from image denoising to crack path calculation. Particularly important is the noise reduction and the shadow elimination, because otherwise, misclassification of pixels occurs. Even that in about 93% of the images analized (around 1200) we were able to eliminate shadows correctly, there are some cases where different cracks are detected as one crack (they are erroneously joined), and other cases where one crack is divided into two cracks. We are analyzing how can we improve the accuracy of the method when detecting cracks by improving the removing of the shadows. Another thing to work on, is that grain boundaries are sometimes confused with cracks; however this can be easily identified because the cracks are small in length; that is, visually one can observe like a discontinuous crack (like a dotted line).

Acknowledgment. The authors would like to thank to Dr. Narciso Acuña, researcher who is investigating the properties of the materials, for his valuable contributions for this work. We also would like to thank to Universidad Anahuac-Mayab for supporting this work.

References

1. Rosell, G., Mendez, J.: Bone cement: prevention of exposure to its components. Technical notes. National Institute of Health and Safety at Work, Spain (2009)
2. Quesada, F., Charris, J., Perez, J.: Ensayos de fatiga en viga rotativa para determinar la Constante de Miner del acero Aisi 1045. Prospectiva 6(2) (2008)
3. Nicholson, D., Ni, P., Ahn, Y.: Probabilistic theory for mixed mode fatigue crack growth in brittle plazes with random cracks. Engineering Fracture Mechanics 66, 305–320 (2000)
4. Meyer, S., Bruckner-Foit, A., Moslang, A., Diegele, E.: Stochastic simulation model for microcracks in a martensitic steel. Computational Materials Science 26, 102–110 (2003)
5. Heron, E., Walsh, C.: A continuous latent spatial model for crack initiation in bone cement. Applied Statistics 57, 25–42 (2008)
6. Chiquet, J., Limnios, N., Eid, M.: Piecewise deterministic Markov processes applied to fatigue crack growth modelling. Journal of Statistical Planning and Inference 139(5), 1657–1667 (2009)
7. Otsu, N.: A Threshold Selection Method from Gray-Level Histograms. IEEE Transactions on System, Man, and Cybernetics SMC-9(1) (1979)

Mobile and Context-Aware Grocery Shopping to Promote Active Aging

Netzahualcoyotl Hernández[1], Carlos Refugio[1], Monica Tentori[1], Jesus Favela[1], and Sergio Ochoa[2]

[1] Computer Science Department, CICESE Research Center, Ensenada, México
[2] Computer Science Department, Universidad de Chile, Santiago, Chile
{hcruz,hflores,mtentori,favela}@cicese.mx,
sochoa@dd.uchile.cl

Abstract. Active aging aims at promoting physical activity, socialization and participation in society as a mechanism to improve physical and mental health. We explore the use of a mobile, context-aware application to help elders transform their grocery shopping experience into an activity that promotes active aging. We describe the design and formative evaluation of WaSSAA, a mobile application to persuade elders to exercise and socialize while sharing grocery prices and promoting "smart" grocery shopping. WaSSAA uses location information to promote social encounters and to ask shoppers to gather price information for fellow users, and the accelerometer to estimate physical activity and reward its user. Results of a formative evaluation of the usefulness of WaSSAA with 16 elders shows that older adults are aware and sensitive to grocery prices and find the application useful to guide them when comparing prices during grocery shopping. They also perceive grocery shopping as a social activity and welcome WaSSAA's services to encourage in-person encounters.

Keywords: Active aging, Price sensitivity, Grocery shopping, Social shopping.

1 Introduction

Research in Ambient Assisted Living (AAL) has focused on developing intelligent environments that can assist older adults and people with disabilities to compensate their functional limitations to complete activities of daily living [1]. As stated by the Active Ageing policy framework, AAL should extend its scope beyond caring for people with disability to prevention and wellness management [2].

Active aging aims at promoting social participation and health in order to enhance our quality of life as we age. Its objective is to preserve the physical and mental health of individuals by keeping them physically and socially active, and by promoting their social, economic, and cultural participation in the community [3]. Active aging changes the way we conceive the relation between aging and health. Rather than looking at older adults as individuals with deteriorating health, it aims at maintaining their physical and mental health trough the adoption of healthy habits and behaviors.

Our aim is to design technology that encourages older adults to exercise, socialize, and actively participate in their communities. We decided to focus our attention in an activity that most adults perform regularly, that has an important social component and which involves walking, a kind of physical activity that physicians recommend to

C. Nugent, A. Coronato, and J. Bravo (Eds.): IWAAL 2013, LNCS 8277, pp. 71–79, 2013.
© Springer International Publishing Switzerland 2013

older adults due to its effectiveness and simplicity. The activity we selected is grocery shopping. Grocery shopping is an Instrumental Activity of Daily Living (IADL), thus it is associated to independent living [4]. It is an activity usually performed several times a week, which takes a considerable amount of time. It involves some degree of physical exercise, particularly when the person has to walk more than a few blocks to go shopping. The activity also has a social component, it requires the interaction with other people, and older adults often go with someone else to the grocery store.

We aim to promote physical exercise, socialization, and community engagement by promoting older adults to do "smart" grocery shopping and save money while doing this. There is evidence in the literature that older adults tend to be aware of the price of groceries and sensitive to its fluctuations [5]. Thus, they might be willing to walk a bit more if they can save. In addition, we could motivate them to walk to the store in order to collect price information that could be used by fellow shoppers, thus helping them contribute to their community.

There are applications that provide some of the services we just described, for example LiveCompare [6] provides services to identify the most economic grocery store, and iGrocery [7] additionally provides nutrition information. However, apps like LiveCompare, iGrocery, and GroceryiQ [8] limited their services to store shopping lists without providing information about social interaction opportunity when shopping, providing a partial solution to the issues of socialization and health care that have emerged in the research conducted in this study.

This paper reports a qualitative study (section 2) to inform the design (section 3) of a mobile and context-aware application for active aging supporting grocery shopping (section 4); and results of 3 focus groups conducted in 3 different countries to validate our design and gather further insights of its utility and adoption (section 5).

2   Understanding the Shopping Practices of Older Adults

For 3 months, we conducted a qualitative study to understand older adults shopping strategies. We conducted 5 semi-structured interviews for an average of around 44 minutes each, with 5 older adults. We complemented our interviews with 3 hours of passive observation of older adults in two naturalistic conditions: (1) exercising in a park and in a social welfare group, and (2) shopping groceries at a major grocery store. We used affinity diagramming and techniques to derive axial coding from grounded theory to analyze all the transcribed interviews and observations [9].

We found that our informants are quite sensitive to grocery prices, which is consistent with findings reported in the literature [10-12]. Price was their main criteria in deciding where to shop, with distance to the shop being second. All informants reported using a memory aid to assist their shopping, mostly in the form of a grocery list. They are also aware of discounts and offers, information they gather from TV ads, publicity in the supermarkets and friends. Our informants usually walk to the store unless they have to go far or return with many groceries, in which case they drove or took a taxi back home. When accompanied by a friend or family member they usually took more time shopping and walking around in the store.

3   Designing a Grocery Shopping Application for Active Aging

Following an interactive user-centered design methodology we used the results of the qualitative study to iteratively design a low-fidelity prototype of a mobile grocery shopping application. The design of the prototype was discussed during several design sessions, in two of which, one of the informants participated.

Our approach relies on using mobile technologies and pervasive sensing as constructs to transform the activity of grocery shopping into an engaging activity to promote active aging. With the system an older adult may exercise and socialize while shopping for groceries. The system should address the following requirements:

- **Provide means to easily consult and edit a grocery list.** Older adults use grocery lists as an aid to plan their grocery shopping.
- **Enable context-aware grocery store suggestions.** We found out older adults decisions to where to go for grocery shopping are context sensitive. Therefore a system should take advantage of the relevant context based on distance, cost, and the amount of items to carry, so older adults could make an informed decision.
- **Motivate and ease the capture of food prices and recommendations with minimal effort from older adults.** Older adults could capture recommendations to benefit others and the system should provide incentives to share food prices.
- **Promote exercising and socialization.** As exercising and socialization are key features for active aging the system should enable the automatic recognition of the amount of physical activity performed by the user and monitor the location of friends to timely suggest a user when to socialize and exercise.

To show how WaSSAA (Walk, Save, and Share for Active Aging) could be used when shopping groceries we present a scenario of the use of the system.

Miguel is 72 years-old; he is retired and lives alone since his wife died two years ago. After breakfast he updates his grocery list using WaSSAA on his smartphone (Figure 2 left). He then looks at the alternatives WaSSAA presents to him as grocery shopping plans. This information includes the different markets in the vicinity Miguel could visit, the potential cost of buying the items in his grocery list at each market, and how much exercise he could potentially do by walking towards each market (Figure 2 middle). Miguel uses this information to decide to go to market ABC, which has the lowest total cost for the items in his shopping list. He selects this option, indicating that he is planning to walk to the store in approximately 15 minutes. WaSSAA notifies Miguel's grocery shopping plan to his friends. Alejandro, a neighbor and friend of Miguel sees this message and decides to join Miguel. Alejandro uses WaSSAA to send a message notifying Miguel he will be at his home in about 10 minutes to accompany him to the store. They both walk to the store talking about the soccer match of the night before. Once in the store, WaSSAA notifies them both that they have received an award for walking 7 blocks, and an invitation to capture the current price of two products in that store: apples and milk. Knowing that providing this information will give them points they can later redeem for products in the store, they decide to capture the prices using WaSSAA. When walking back home they pass in front of their friend's Carmen home, WaSSAA notifies Carmen that Miguel and Alejandro are nearby and she comes out to greet them.

4   Walk, Save and Share for Active Aging: The WaSSAA App

The design of WaSSAA is based on a three-tier client-server architecture (Fig. 1). The data layer records information about users, groceries, prices, and rewards in a relational database. The business layer includes the application logic, such as creating recommendations for grocery shopping and deciding what product prices might need to be updated. Both these layers are executed in the WaSSAA server. Finally, the presentation layer runs in the mobile phone and displays recommendations, the shopping list, and rewards to the user. We next describe the WaSSAA components.

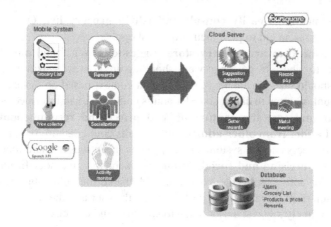

Fig. 1. Architecture of WaSSAA

WaSSAA Mobile Client

Grocery List. The user uses this module to update his shopping list. This can be done directly on the mobile device or through a web page, thus allowing other household members to add items to the shopping list. The recommendation module uses this information to present the user with shopping alternatives and suggestions.

Price Collector. This component implements two alternative mechanisms to gather price information using the mobile device: (1) *voice command* when activated records audio that is interpreted using the *Google Speech API*; and (2) *typing text* that allows the user to capture the price of the product by directly typing the amount.

The price information captured by the user is stored in the server. A tuple: {product, price, confidence} is stored in the database. The Confidence is a value from 1 to 5, calculated from the reliability of the user, determined based on its history record, variations in prices reported and how recently was the price updated. When a user captures a new price, his rewards are updated in the database.

Rewards Module. It is used to inform the user of the rewards he has obtained by capturing prices using the application. It keeps information about the number of users who have used prices updated by this user.

Activity Monitor. This component uses the accelerometer in the smartphone to estimate number of steps the older adult walks, giving him rewards when reaching certain thresholds.

Socialization Module. It is used to inform the user of opportunities for social encounters with the user's social network. When the user consults this information, a query is formulated to the Match meeting component in the server.

WaSSAA Server

Recommendation Module. This component locates stores in the vicinity and uses distance to the home of the user, and price information to generate a list of alternative shopping plans. The module uses the Foursquare API to locate relevant stores. Shopping plans are sent to the mobile device and presented as alternatives to the user.

Database. It uses a relational database to record information about users, products, prices and rewards.

4.1   Using WaSSAA

To show how the components of the architecture interact among them, we revisit the scenario described in Section 3. Miguel regularly opens the mobile app to update his shopping list (Figure 2a). When he plans to go shopping he selects the option that brings him the alternative sites with the total cost and approximate amount of walking involved in shopping at each site (Figure 2b). To provide this information the app uses the Foursquare API to consult grocery stores in the vicinity and the database of products and prices stored in the server. Once Miguel selects the alternative he plans to follow the system asks him if he wants to notify his friends that he is planning to go shopping and if this is the case to indicate the approximate time when he is planning to leave (now; in 15mins; in 30mins; in 1hour). In this case Miguel indicates that he plans to go shopping in 15 minutes and the friends he wants the system to notify (Figure 2c). Alejandro receives this message and WaSSAA allows him to notify Miguel that he will go to his house for both of them to walk together to the store.

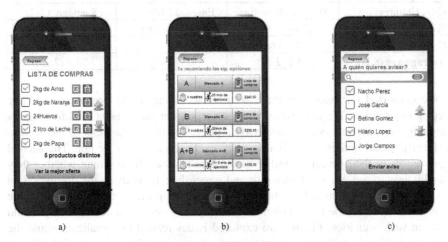

Fig. 2. The WaSSAA mobile app: a. Grocery shopping list; b. Alternative markets to shop with price and exercise information; c. Notifying friends of a trip to the shop.

When the users approach the store WaSSAA automatically checks-in for them in Foursqure. Aware of their location, the system asks them to collect prices of certain products. Finally, the system rewards Miguel and Alejandro for the prices they have collected and the amount of physical exercise they made by walking to the store.

5   Formative Evaluation of WaSSAA

Three focus group sessions with older adults where conducted to evaluate WaSSAA. We aimed at validating the assumptions behind the design of WaSSAA, its utility and ease of use. The protocol for the focus group included 34 semi-structured questions and two scenarios one illustrating the use of WaSSAA (as described above), and the same situation without the system. The sessions lasted about 90 minutes.

The questionnaire had 5 sections: Incentives (habits and motivation); Exercising (frequency of physical activity); Grocery shopping (routines, price sensitivity, transportation); Technology use (use of smartphones and the WaSSAA app).

A total of 16 older adults participated in the focus group sessions, with an average age of 71. Participants reported having the habit of shopping, no difficulty walking, experience using smartphones more than 6 months, and no problems reading and understanding smartphones' notifications. As shown in Table 1, the focus groups where conducted in three different Spanish-speaking countries, one in a small city, a second one in a medium-size city and the third one in a large city. This was done to validate our design across different demographics and conditions, and to identify differences in the way in which our informants perceived the utility of the application.

Table 1. Focus group sessions to evaluate WaSSAA

	Focus group A	Focus group B	Focus group C
No. of participants	5	6	5
City, Country	Bolivar, Argentina	Ensenada, Mexico	Santiago, Chile
Size of the city	Small (30k)	Medium (500k)	Large (5,000k)
Gender	(2 male; 3 female)	(1 male; 5 female)	(2 male; 3 female)
Average age (S.D)	74.2 (2.22)	65 (2.94)	73.8 (7.35)

We organized our results in three sections according to the organization of the focus group session. We first explored the strategies the participants used for grocery shopping, their awareness and sensitivity to price, and their awareness of the need to perform physical activity and weather they exercised regularly or not. The second topic relates to their perceived utility of the WaSSAA application and whether they found it easy to use. We used scenarios and screenshots to motivate the discussion on this topic. They were asked to put themselves in the position of the person in the scenario, to interpret the information provided by the system and decision they would make in such scenarios. Finally, we explored issues related to socialization and the various ways in which the participants perceived grocery shopping as a social activity.

5.1 Price Awareness and Sensitivity

All the participants divide their grocery shopping in one major shopping trip that is made once every one to four weeks, with more frequent trips (daily in many cases), mostly to shop for perishable food items such as fruit or bread. It was common practice to go to a larger market for the main shopping and to local markets for the more frequent trips. They would usually drive or take a taxi for the major shopping trip. In both, group B and C, the main buying criteria was to obtain good quality products at the best price possible. They were well aware of the prices of the products they regularly buy and tend to compare prices and be aware of discounts mostly to advertisement and comments from friends.

"I go to the street market because the fruit and vegetables are fresh and very cheap, sometimes the tomato costs 5 or 6 pesos, the strawberry at 15 pesos and 1 kilo of cucumber for 10 pesos" (Participant, Group B).

In contrast, the participants in group A emphasized the social aspect of grocery shopping. They normally shop in the same place and were unaware of price differences. They are friends with the owners of the markets they visit, and keep shopping there out of solidarity with these small shops, and because they appreciate the social interaction involved in grocery shopping. In addition, the owners and employees know them well and offer them the products they know they like.

"They have the brands I buy, the cashiers are very polite, it is nearby, the butcher is my friend, the owners live in the town" (Participant, Group A).

All participants agreed that if the cost of a product increases sharply they will look for cheaper alternatives or even stop buying the product altogether. Thus, they are clearly sensitive to price.

All participants were aware of the importance of performing physical exercise for their health, yet only one participant in each focus group exercised regularly. Participants in groups B and C considered walking to go grocery shopping as a form of exercise, while those in group A did not.

5.2 Utility and Ease of Use of WaSSAA

We found that all participants elaborate some kind of list of groceries and products to buy, and considered the list provided by WaSSAA to be easy to use. They all agreed that the service to compare was useful and they were in general surprised that a mobile phone could be capable of integrating such service. Participants in group B and C even suggested that having this information could make them change their shopping habits. When asked if they would change anything in the app to make it more useful or easy to use they made no suggestions. Apparently their lack of familiarity with this type of devices and applications made it difficult for them to criticize the interface. On the other hand, they all agreed that the information was clear and easy to understand.

With respect to using the application to collect price information, they were all reluctant to do that, even when they were told that this information would be useful to other shoppers. Only when they were told that they could obtain a retribution for doing this, in the form of discounts of coupons for grocery shopping, they expressed enthusiasm with the idea.

5.3   Socialization Strategies Associated to Grocery Shopping

The participants in all three groups look for opportunities to socialize with friends and family. They all consider grocery shopping as a social activity, particularly those in group A, who are friends with the owners of the shops they frequent. All of them mentioned that they sometimes call friends to let them know of discounts they have seen in a market or advertised elsewhere. As one of the participants mentioned:

"The orange for example has been at less than 4 pesos per kilo, the good one (without seeds)... as far as I remember I have told this to more than two people and it seems that they have taken advantage [of this deal]". (Participant, Group B)

Frequently they go shopping with a friend, with those who have a car often inviting those who do not, when they go shopping to a larger, more distant shop. They appreciate the fact that grocery shopping keeps them socially and physically active.

"[if there were home delivery] I wouldn't use it, because I would have a lot of free time. When you go to the market you walk, talk with other people, see different things.. you distract and relax yourself. I don't want to be in-doors at home all day".

They all appreciated the services offered by WaSSAA to promote socialization by coordinating the shopping sessions as illustrated in the scenario described. A participant in group C, who has some difficulties walking due to a hip problem, even suggested that she would like to know if friends are passing in front of her house to go outside and chat with them.

6   Conclusions

In this paper, we describe the design and formative evaluation of WaSSAA, a mobile and context-aware tool that promotes active aging by transforming the shopping experience of older adults. WaSSAA takes into consideration the distance, cost, and time for travelling to the market as contextual information to help older adults make an informed decision to where to go grocery-shopping balancing savings, exercising and socialization. While there are some mobile apps that support certain aspects of grocery shopping, such as managing a shopping list (iGrocery [7] or Grocery iQ), or monitoring shopping time [13], and many others that monitor physical activity, none of these efforts aim at supporting active aging through grocery shopping

The primary contribution of this work was to articulate and explore the design space of using mobile and context-aware computing to promote active aging. Our results indicate our approach is feasible and perceived as useful by older adults of three different countries. We plan to fully develop the system and conduct a deployment evaluation to see its impact in everyday grocery shopping practices.

References

[1] Gersch, M., Lindert, R., Hewing, M.: AAL-business models: Different Prospects for the Successful Implementation of Innovative Services in the Primary and Secondary Healthcare Market. In: AALIANCE Conference, Malaga, Spain (2010)

[2] WHO (World Health Organization), Active ageing: a policy framework, WHO/NMH/NPH/02.8. WHO, Geneva (2002)

[3] Wiederhold, B.K., Riva, G., Graffigna, G.: Ensuring the best care for our increasing aging population: health engagement and positive technology can help patients achieve a more active role in future healthcare. Cyberpsychol. Behav. Soc. Netw. 16(6), 411–412 (2013)

[4] Lawton, M.P., Brody, E.M.: Assessment of older people: Self-maintaining and instrumental activities of daily living. Gerontologist 9, 179–186 (1969)

[5] Zeitham, V.A., Fuerst, W.L.: Age Differences in Response to Grocery Store Price Information. Journal of Consumer Affairs 17(2), 402–420 (1983)

[6] Deng, L., Cox, L.P.: LiveCompare: grocery bargain hunting through participatory sensing. In: Proceedings of the 10th Workshop on Mobile Computing Systems and Applications (HotMobile 2009). ACM, New York (2009)

[7] Sangeetha, S., Prashant, N., Abdelsalam, H.: iGrocer: a ubiquitous and pervasive smart grocery shopping system. In: ACM Symposium on Applied Computing, pp. 645–652 (2003)

[8] GroceryiQ. Shopping list app, http://www.groceryiq.com/ (visited on September 2013)

[9] Beyer, H., Holtzblatt, K.: Contextual design: defining customer centered systems. Morgan Kaufmann, San Francisco (1998)

[10] Kenesei, A., Todd, S.: The Use of Price in the Purchase Decision. Journal of Empirical Generalisations in Marketing Science 8(1) (2003)

[11] Tongren, H.N.: Determinant Behavior Characteristics of Older Consumers. Journal of Consumer Affairs 22(1), 136–157 (1988)

[12] Sirvanci, M.: An Empirical Study of Price Thresholds and Price Sensitivity. Journal of Applied Business Research 9(2), 43–49 (1993)

[13] You, C.-W., et al.: Using Mobile Phones to Monitor Shopping Time at Physical Stores. IEEE Pervasive Computing 10(2), 37–43 (2011)

Handling Displacement Effects in On-Body Sensor-Based Activity Recognition

Oresti Baños*, Miguel Damas, Héctor Pomares, and Ignacio Rojas

Department of Computer Architecture and Computer Technology, Research Center
for Information and Communications Technologies of the University of Granada
(CITIC-UGR)
C/Periodista Daniel Saucedo Aranda s/n, 18071 Granada, Spain
{oresti,mdamas,hector,irojas}@ugr.es
http://citic.ugr.es

Abstract. So far little attention has been paid to activity recognition systems limitations during out-of-lab daily usage. Sensor displacement is one of these major issues, particularly deleterious for inertial on-body sensing. The effect of the displacement normally translates into a drift on the signal space that further propagates to the feature level, thus modifying the expected behavior of the predefined recognition systems. On the use of several sensors and diverse motion-sensing modalities, in this paper we compare two fusion methods to evaluate the importance of decoupling the combination process at feature and classification levels under realistic sensor configurations. In particular a 'feature fusion' and a 'multi-sensor hierarchical-classifier' are considered. The results reveal that the aggregation of sensor-based decisions may overcome the difficulties introduced by the displacement and confirm the gyroscope as possibly the most displacement-robust sensor modality.

Keywords: Sensor displacement, Sensor network, Sensor fusion, Activity recognition, Human Behavior, Motion sensors.

1 Introduction

The development of systems and mechanisms capable of analyzing the human behavior has attracted tremendous attention during the last few years. The potential of activity recognition (AR) applications supports such interest and evidences their wide possibilities. Monitoring and identifying people routines or actions may be used in domestic contexts to avoid or alert from risk situations such as falls or faintings or promote healthier lifestyles through personalized guidelines and recommendations [1]. Workplace environments may also leverage the use of AR systems to increase for example the productivity in industrial maintenance or reinforce safety procedures [14]. Field-specific systems may also help high-level athletes to improve their performance or scores as well as amateurs to get insights about how to make faster progresses within a particular sport discipline [11].

---

* Corresponding author.

C. Nugent, A. Coronato, and J. Bravo (Eds.): IWAAL 2013, LNCS 8277, pp. 80–87, 2013.
© Springer International Publishing Switzerland 2013

Although there are hundreds of contributions that tackle the activity recognition problem, the maturity of this field is still reduced due to numerous unresolved issues related to systems reliability, robustness, pervasiveness and seamless of usage. One of these unresolved matters is sensor displacement, which is particularly critical in on-body inertial-sensing. Body sensors are usually located in specific places recommended by the manufacturer, however their use under daily living circumstances demonstrate that wrong attachments, loss of fitting or abrupt movements frequently drive to sensors de-positioning. Only a few contributions have analyzed issues in this regard. Kunze *et al.* described a first attempt to self-characterize sensors' on-body placement [9] and orientation [10] from the acceleration analysis during walking. They also demonstrated the effect of rotations and displacement in accelerometers, and proposed a way to partially deal with them through the use of additional sensor modalities [8]. These heuristic methods are coupled to the assumption that the user performs the specific activities required at some point, which nevertheless might not always be guaranteed. Foerster *et al.* [7] studied the possibility of systems self-calibration through the adjustment of the classifier decision boundaries. This supports tracking the changes experimented in the feature space due to the sensor displacement. Similarly in [5] the authors proposed a method to compensate the data distribution shift caused by sensor displacements through the use of an expectation-maximization algorithm and covariance shift analysis.

As an alternative, sensor fusion may be encountered to cope with displacement effects. A key advantage is that identifying the failure sources is not necessarily required to compensate the associated errors in the activity recognition process. Just a few previous works addressed this problem in this regard. Zappi *et al.* [15] showed a significant tolerance increase by using a large set of sensors in combination with majority voting or naive Bayes decision fusion models. A more sophisticated scheme is presented in [13] which attempts to detect anomalies and potential affected sensors in order to remove them from the sensor ecology. Similarly, in [3] the authors applied sensor fusion for dealing with synthetically induced sensor anomalies.

In this work we apply two fusion models that are ultimately compared in terms of accuracy and robustness. The models are tested on a realistic dataset especially intended to benchmark techniques that deal with the effects of sensor displacement and de-positioning in activity recognition. The rest of the paper is organized as follows. In Section 2 the effects of displacement on inertial monitoring are described. Section 3 briefly introduces the AR methodology while Section 4 presents the experimental setup. Results and discussion are provided in Section 5. Finally, Section 6 summarizes main conclusions.

2   Sensor Displacement Effects

The concept of sensor displacement (in application to inertial on-body sensing) may be understood as the combination of two transformations: rotations and translations. According to the physics of the rigid body, rotations refer to the circular movements that the sensor experiences around its rotation axes or upon itself. Translations correspond to the movements of the sensor from a given position to another distant position through a specific direction.

Sensor displacement applies to each inertial sensing modality (acceleration, rate of turn, magnetic field) to a different extent. Thus for example, acceleration is especially sensitive to rotations. Rotations determine a change in the sensor local frame of reference with respect to its original spatial distribution. This causes a shift in the direction of the gravitational component with respect to the sensor reference frame. The effect of translations is normally more dependent on the initial and end position as well as the magnitude of the acceleration experienced by the sensor. More robust to displacement anomalies are gyroscopes, which are minimally affected by rotations along their rotation axis and translations along the same body limb. Magnetic field measurements are also affected by rotations and to a lower extent by translations when assuming no gimbal lock degeneration.

Sensor displacement normally leads to a new signal space. In this new space the sensor readings likely differ with respect to those expected from a default or predefined sensor placement. These changes propagate through the different stages of the activity recognition chain (Section 3), thus affecting the inference process. An example of such effects is depicted in Figure 1. Here, a sensor displacement unintentionally introduced by the user when self-attaching the devices (Figure 1(a)) translates into a significant drift at the feature level (Figure 1(b)). Consequently, a model trained under the assumption of an ideal placement of the sensors (and accordingly a bounded feature space) may not normally cope with the variations introduced by the new feature space.

Other factors that also influence the magnitude of the displacement effects are the sensor on-body location (initial and final) and the magnitude of the motion experienced by the affected sensors. Thus for example, the drift may be pronounced when the sensor is displaced from the extreme of a limb (highly motional) to a position closer to the trunk (more limited mobility) when energetic activities are performed. On the contrary, during inactivity or while resting this change may not have appreciable consequences. Therefore, the effects are quite dependent on the particular activities, gestures or movements the user performs.

3   Activity Recognition Methods

Activity recognition approaches normally consist of a set of steps also known as activity recognition chain (an insightful review may be seen in [12]). Given a set of sensors positioned in different parts of the subject's body, these nodes are used to measure the motion experienced by each part. These records are translated into raw unprocessed signals that numerically represent the magnitude measured. Sometimes the signals are filtered out to remove possible anomalies such as electronic noise, however the information loss may be inappropriate in other cases. To capture the dynamics of the movements the signals are further segmented in partitions of a given size, normally through windowing or

(a) Sensor displacement originated during sensor self-placement ($LC_{IDEAL} = LC_{SELF}$, $RC_{IDEAL} \neq RC_{SELF}$)

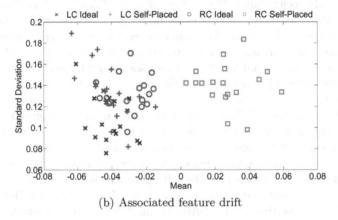

(b) Associated feature drift

Fig. 1. Example of sensor displacement introduced during the user self-placement (a) and its effect at the feature level (b). In this particular example the displacement from the default to the self-placement case applies to the right calf (RC) while the position remains roughly similar for the sensor attached to the left calf (LC). In (b) each mark represents an instance of the 'jump up' activity.

event/activity based techniques. Then a specific set of features are extracted from the data to provide a handler representation of the signals for the pattern recognition stage. A wide range of heuristics, time/frequency domain and other sophisticated mathematical and statistic functions are commonly used. The feature vector is provided as input to the classifier, ultimately yielding the recognized activity.

At this point, two approaches are proposed. The first one, here defined as 'feature fusion' corresponds to the case where all features coming from each individual sensor are combined on a single feature vector. This feature vector inputs a generic reasoning model. The second more sophisticated model [2] uses the individual feature streams extracted from each corresponding sensor and fuses the decisions obtained from the classifiers associated to every sensor. The so-called 'multi-sensor hierarchical classifier' is a technique that takes in the main advantages of hierarchical decision and majority voting models. Considering so, the idea is to give all the decision entities the opportunity to collaborate on the decision making, but ranking the relative importance of each decision through the use of weights based on the classification entities individual performance.

4 Experimental Setup

For the evaluation of the proposed model an activity recognition benchmark dataset is used [4]. This dataset is particularly appropriate for sensor de-positioning analysis because of its diverse displacement modes, amount of subjects and variety of activities. Namely, the dataset comprises motion data (tridimensional acceleration - ACC -, rate of turn - GYR - and magnetic field - MAG -) recorded for 17 volunteers while doing 33 'easy-to-perform' fitness exercises. The activity set defines from cardio-exercises such as running or cycling to general body movements like waist rotations ("hula hoop") or body-specific such as arms or knees bending. These exercises are performed while wearing a set of nine inertial sensors attached to different body parts.

Three scenarios in relation to the sensor displacement concept are considered: "ideal-placement", "self-placement" and "induced-displacement". The ideal-placement corresponds to the default or baseline scenario where the sensors are positioned by the instructor to specific well-identified locations (here on the middle of each limb and the back). A subset of the sensors is asked to be placed by the users themselves for the self-placement scenario, thus introducing a more realistic concept of daily sensor usage. Finally, the induced-displacement (also identified as 'mutual') constitutes the most troublesome scenario since intentional de-positioning of sensors is introduced by the instructor. This is of special interest to bench activity recognition solutions in conditions far from the default setup. These two last scenarios will normally lead to on-body sensor setups that differ with respect to the ideal-placement.

A subset of the original datasets is here considered. Ten of the most representative activities define the evaluation bench ($\{1, 4, 8, 10, 12, 18, 22, 25, 28, 33\}$, see [4] for equivalence). These activities apply to the all three datasets ('ideal', 'self' and 'induced'). Moreover, the experimental set includes the evaluation of each separated sensor modality (i.e., ACC, GYR and MAG) and their combinations. A segmentation process consisting of a non-overlapping sliding window (6 seconds size) is applied to each data stream. Mean, standard deviation, maximum, minimum and mean crossing rate are subsequently calculated for each window during the feature extraction process. C4.5 decision trees [6], which have been extensively and successfully applied in previous activity recognition problems, are used both for the multi-class classifiers and the binary or base classifiers components of the hierarchical approach. For the ideal scenario a tenfold random-partitioning cross validation process is applied across all subjects and activities. This process is repeated 100 times for each method to ensure statistical robustness. For both 'self' and 'induced' cases the procedure consists of testing a system trained in all 'ideal' data on the formers.

5   Results and Discussion

Figure 2 depicts the accuracy results for both feature fusion and multi-sensor hierarchical classifier. The evaluation of the models on the different sensor-placement scenarios (legend) is shown for each sensor modality or combination (X axis). The accuracy results demonstrate that the proposed methods are adequate solutions under the assumption of a fixed sensor setup. Nevertheless, it should be noted that both self-positioning and induced-displacement scenarios introduce a significant drop on the recognition systems performance with respect

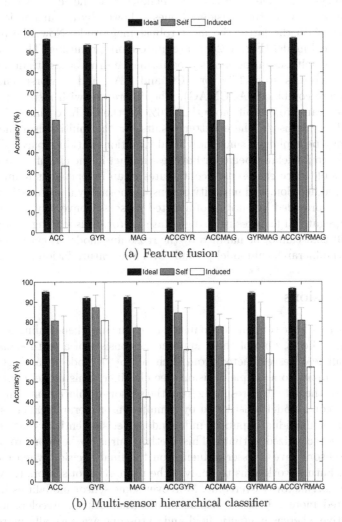

Fig. 2. Accuracy (mean and standard deviation) results from the evaluation of the a) feature fusion and b) multi-sensor hierarchical classifier when tested on the fitness dataset (the top legend identifies the type of sensor placement, see Section 4). Horizontal axis labels correspond to the sensor modalities used during the evaluation.

to the ideal or default scenario, which confirms the effects described in section 2. Clearly, the more profound the displacement applied ('induced' case) the higher the performance drop.

There are significant differences depending on whether the feature fusion or the multi-sensor hierarchical classifier are approached. When using the feature fusion (Figure 2(a)) it can be found differences with respect to the 'ideal' performance and the 'self' scenario that range from approximately 20% in the best case (GYR) to more than 40% at worst (ACC). This is more pronounced for the 'induced' case, where the variations go from 25% for the GYR to 65% again for the ACC based system. Thereby, it can be concluded that the acceleration modality is the most sensitive of the considered ones, followed by the magnetic field and rate of turn, with the latter the most robust magnitude. Now, the results for the hierarchical model (Figure 2(b)) are quite more promising. The comparison of 'ideal' and 'self' scenarios shows a performance drop of less than 5% for the GYR that increases up to 15% for ACC and MAG and at worst reaches 20% when both are combined (ACCMAG). The differences with respect to the 'induced' case spans from a bit more than 10% for the GYR to almost 50% when MAG modality is used. These better results for the multi-sensor hierarchical classifier may be explained since individual variations within a particular sensor with respect to its default behavior have less impact in the classification process. This is possible since each sensor contributes in an independent manner to the final delivered decision, so a majority of sensors (normally unaffected) overcomes the decisions provided by entities of affected sensors. Conversely, feature fusion models aggregate all features in a single data vector, thus leading to a potential feature drift that cannot be handled by the reasoning model. It can be concluded then that the hierarchical model prevails over the feature fusion approach.

6   Conclusions

In this paper we have compared two fusion mechanisms when dealing with sensor displacement effects. One of these approaches consists of a feature fusion that combines all features extracted from each sensor or node in a single feature vector that inputs to a simple decision tree classifier. This model demonstrates to not handle the data drift resulting from the sensors displacement. On the other hand, the second model constituted by a multi-sensor hierarchical classifier uses each sensor as individual inputs to independent decision entities that eventually concur on a recognized activity. This method turns to be more robust since displaced sensors have a lesser influence on the final decision when considered a minority. Future work aims to analyze the proportion of sensors to which the influence is satisfactorily overcome. Moreover some sensor modalities have been demonstrated more robust to displacements than others. Acceleration is the more sensitive whereas magnetic field and gyroscope are normally more robust, especially the latter. Combinations of inertial modalities do not necessarily lead to further improvement but to increase the complexity of the recognition system.

Acknowledgments. Work supported by the HPC-Europa2 (no. 228398) and CICYT SAF2010-20558 projects and the FPU Spanish grant AP2009-2244.

References

1. Albert, M.V., Toledo, S., Shapiro, M., Kording, K.: Using mobile phones for activity recognition in parkinsons patients. Frontiers in Neurology 3(158) (2012)
2. Banos, O., Damas, M., Pomares, H., Rojas, F., Delgado-Marquez, B., Valenzuela, O.: Human activity recognition based on a sensor weighting hierarchical classifier. Soft. Computing 17, 333–343 (2013)
3. Banos, O., Damas, M., Pomares, H., Rojas, I.: On the use of sensor fusion to reduce the impact of rotational and additive noise in human activity recognition. Sensors 12(6), 8039–8054 (2012)
4. Banos, O., Damas, M., Pomares, H., Rojas, I., Attila Toth, M., Amft, O.: A benchmark dataset to evaluate sensor displacement in activity recognition. In: Proceedings of the 2012 ACM Conference on Ubiquitous Computing, UbiComp 2012, pp. 1026–1035. ACM, New York (2012)
5. Chavarriaga, R., Bayati, H., del R. Millán, J.: Unsupervised adaptation for acceleration-based activity recognition: robustness to sensor displacement and rotation. Pers. Ubiquit. Comput., 1–12 (2012)
6. Duda, R.O., Hart, P.E., Stork, D.G.: Pattern Classification, 2nd edn. Wiley-Interscience (2000)
7. Förster, K., Roggen, D., Tröster, G.: Unsupervised classifier self-calibration through repeated context occurences: Is there robustness against sensor displacement to gain? In: Proc. 13th IEEE Int. Symposium on Wearable Computers (ISWC), Linz, Austria, pp. 77–84. IEEE Press (September 2009)
8. Kunze, K., Lukowicz, P.: Dealing with sensor displacement in motion-based on-body activity recognition systems. In: 10th International Conference on Ubiquitous Computing, Seoul, South Korea, pp. 20–29. ACM Press (September 2008)
9. Kunze, K., Lukowicz, P., Junker, H., Tröster, G.: Where am I: Recognizing on-body positions of wearable sensors. In: Strang, T., Linnhoff-Popien, C. (eds.) LoCA 2005. LNCS, vol. 3479, pp. 264–275. Springer, Heidelberg (2005)
10. Kunze, K., Lukowicz, P., Partridge, K., Begole, B.: Which way am i facing: Inferring horizontal device orientation from an accelerometer signal. In: 13th IEEE Int. Symposium on Wearable Computers (ISWC), Linz, Austria, pp. 149–150. IEEE Press (September 2009)
11. Kusserow, M., Amft, O., Gubelmann, H., Troester, G.: Arousal pattern analysis of an olympic champion in ski jumping. Sports Technology 3(3), 192–203 (2010)
12. Lara, O., Labrador, M.: A survey on human activity recognition using wearable sensors. IEEE Communications Surveys Tutorials PP(99), 1–18 (2012)
13. Sagha, H., del R. Millan, J., Chavarriaga, R.: Detecting and rectifying anomalies in opportunistic sensor networks. In: 8th Int. Conf. on Networked Sensing Systems, Penghu, Taiwan, pp. 162–167. IEEE Press (June 2011)
14. Stiefmeier, T., Roggen, D., Ogris, G., Lukowicz, P., Tröster, G.: Wearable activity tracking in car manufacturing. IEEE Pervasive Computing 7(2), 42–50 (2008)
15. Zappi, P., Stiefmeier, T., Farella, E., Roggen, D., Benini, L., Troster, G.: Activity recognition from on-body sensors by classifier fusion: sensor scalability and robustness. In: 3rd International Conference on Intelligent Sensors, Sensor Networks and Information, Melbourne, Australia, pp. 281–286. IEEE Press (December 2007)

Application of a Cluster-Based Classifier Ensemble to Activity Recognition in Smart Homes

Anna Jurek, Yaxin Bi, Christopher Nugent, and Shengli Wu

School of Computing and Mathematics, University of Ulster,
Jordanstown, Shore Road, Newtownabbey, Co. Antrim, UK, BT37 0QB
jurek-a@email.ulster.ac.uk,
{y.bi,cd.nugent,s.wu1}@ulster.ac.uk

Abstract. An increasingly popular technique of monitoring activities within a smart environment involves the use of sensor technologies. With such an approach complex constructs of data are generated which subsequently require the use of activity recognition techniques to infer the underlying activity. The assignment of sensor data to one from a possible set of predefined activities can essentially be considered as a classification task. In this study, we propose the application of a cluster-based classifier ensemble method to the activity recognition problem, as an alternative to single classification models. Experimental evaluation has been conducted on publicly available sensor data collected over a period of 26 days from a single person apartment. Two types of sensor data representation have been considered, namely numeric and binary. The results show that the ensemble method performs with accuracies of 94.2% and 97.5% for numeric and binary data, respectively. These results outperformed a range of single classifiers.

Keywords: Activity recognition, classifier ensembles, smart homes.

1   Introduction

A popular approach in healthcare for assessing physical and cognitive well-being is through monitoring of users' activities of daily living (ADL). ADLs are activities which are performed daily, for example toileting, grooming, cooking or undertaking light house work. Monitoring such activities can provide useful information which can be used to either recognise an emergency situation or to identify behavioural changes over time. The problem of activity monitoring has been addressed by many studies over the years [1, 2, 3]. One of the key components of an activity recognition system is the use of sensor-based technology [2]. An environment can be equipped with sensors which have the ability to record a person's interaction within the environment itself, for example, recording whenever a cupboard is open or closed or the turning on or off of a domestic appliance. Based on the interactions captured it is possible to detect the change of state associated with an object/region within the environment. From a data analysis perspective it is therefore possible to infer from the change of a sensor's state that a person in the environment has interacted with a

C. Nugent, A. Coronato, and J. Bravo (Eds.): IWAAL 2013, LNCS 8277, pp. 88–95, 2013.

specific object. The output from such a sensorised environment is a stream of sensor activations that have occurred within a period of time. Analysis of the data can lead to the recognition of the activities being performed. From a computational perspective there are two main challenges to overcome. The first is related to the partitioning of the stream of data obtained from the sensors into segments which represent each of the activities [3]. Each activity is composed of a combination of actions, such as taking a cup from a cupboard and pouring water from a kettle. The second challenge relates to recognizing which of the predefined activities is represented by a given segmented stream of actions [4]. In other words, it can be regarded as a classification process of an instance representing a string of sensor activations into one of the classes representing activities such as cooking dinner or preparing a drink. It has been the focus of the current study to address the latter challenge with the aim of improving the overall accuracy of classification.

2   Relevant Work

A number of approaches to activity recognition, based on processing data obtained through low-level sensors, have been explored. They can be generally categorized as data-driven approaches and knowledge-driven approaches. In the former the most popular techniques adopted are classification models based on probabilistic reasoning for example Naïve Bayes [4], Hidden Markov Models (HMMs) [5], Conditional Random Fields (CRF) [11] and Partially Observable Markov Process (POMDP) [14]. Other algorithms such as Decision Trees [6] or Neural Networks [7] have also been considered. In the aforementioned studies these approaches have been reported as being successful, however, they require a large number of training examples. Within the application domain of smart environments there is, however, a lack of large annotated data sets. From a knowledge driven perspective the most popular approaches applied have been based on logical modelling [8] or evidential theory [1]. Knowledge-driven approaches do not require large data sets for training purposes, however, elicitation of the knowledge from the domain experts can be a challenging process.

As previously mentioned a large number of studies have been undertaken to improve the performance on the underlying approach to activity recognition. In this research it is hypothesized that ensemble methods could have an advantage over a single model applied to the problem of activity recognition. A classifier ensemble is a group of classifiers which are combined in some manner to produce, as an output, a consensus decision while classifying an unseen pattern [9]. The individual classifiers, which are combined to build the ensemble, are referred to as base classifiers. The main goal of building a classifier ensemble is to provide an improvement of classification performance in comparison to any single base classifier considered in isolation. Following the initial process of creating a collection of base classifiers the next step in the ensemble method is to combine the results obtained from each of the individual base classifiers. This combination process produces the final output and decision of the ensemble. Applying a number of different experts and averaging their decision decreases the risk of selecting the wrong classifier, from which a decision is to be made. Given that some activities may be represented by very similar sensor readings, for example preparing dinner or breakfast, it is beneficial to obtain a range of different opinions rather than applying a single model. In addition, some representation of activities may be very confusing given different human behaviours. For example, two activities may happen at the same time, or they can be interleaved. Representation of such an event may be classified as one of the two activities, depending on the subset of sensors (features) that are considered whilst making the decision. In most cases it is difficult to deal with such cases with a single classifier. Obtaining different opinions, for example, from classifiers trained with different subsets of features, may offer a better solution. In this work we propose a Cluster-Based Classifier Ensemble (CBCE) approach, which has already been presented as an effective classification technique [10], as an alternative approach for the purposes of activity recognition.

3   Cluster-Based Classifier Ensemble

With the CBCE approach a collection of clusters built on a training set is considered as one base classifier [10]. In the classification process a new instance is assigned to its closest cluster from each collection. The final decision is made based on the class labels of the instances from all the selected clusters. The CBCE approach has been previously evaluated on open data sets from the machine learning domain, however, it has not been previously applied within the field of activity recognition.

3.1   Creating Base Classifiers

To obtain a set of different base classifiers (collections of clusters), the clustering process is performed a number of times whilst varying two parameters. The first parameter varied is a subset of attributes applied while calculating the distance between 2 instances. The second parameter varied is the number of clusters generated in the clustering process.

The generation of a single base classifier can be presented as a 3 step process. In Step 1, the subset of features and the number of clusters that are going to be considered in the clustering process are selected randomly. In Step 2 all instances from the training set are divided into clusters according to the selected subset of features. As an output from this process a collection of clusters, which is considered as one base classifier, is obtained. For each cluster in the collection its centroid is calculated. It is assumed that each cluster supports one or more classes depending on the instances it contains. For example, if there is one instance assigned to class c in a cluster, we say that this cluster provides a degree of support to class c. The level of support allocated for a class is dependent on the number of instances from this class and the total number of instances that belong to the cluster. In Step 3 a matrix A_k, referred to as a support matrix, is constructed, where each row refers to one cluster and each column refers to one class. The values in the matrix represent the support given for each class by each of the clusters and are calculated as in Equation 1. N_{ij} represents the number of instances in cluster i that belong to class j and N_i represent the total number of instances in cluster i. M refers to the number of classes in the classification problem being considered. The entire process is repeated K times, where K refers to the size of the ensemble required.

$$A_k[i,j] = \begin{cases} \dfrac{N_{ij} - \dfrac{N_i}{M}}{N_i - \dfrac{N_i}{M}} & if \quad N_{ij} - \dfrac{N_i}{M} \geq 0 \\[4ex] \dfrac{N_{ij} - \dfrac{N_i}{M}}{\dfrac{N_i}{M}} & if \quad otherwise \end{cases} \tag{1}$$

3.2   Combining Base Classifier Outputs

The classification of a new instance can be presented as a 3 Step process. In Step 1, following the presentation of a new instance x the closest cluster from each collection, represented by one row of the matrix, is selected. The selection is performed based on the distance between the new instance and the centroid of the cluster. While calculating the Euclidean distance for each centroid only the subset of features applied in the clustering process is considered. Each of the selected clusters provides a level of support for each of the classes represented by values in the respective row from the support matrix. In Step 2, for each class c_j, the support provided by all selected clusters is combined through application of Equation 2:

$$ExSupp(c_j) = \sum_{k=1}^{K} \begin{cases} e^{\frac{A_k[i_k,j]}{1+d(x,x^k)}} & if \quad A_k[i_k,j] > -1 \\[2ex] 0 & otherwise \end{cases} \tag{2}$$

where i_k is the row from matrix A_k representing the selected cluster, x_k refers to the centroid of the selected cluster and d represents the Euclidean distance metric. In Step 3 the class with the highest support is selected as the final decision.

One of the issues in sensor-based activity recognition is related with a situation where the same activity can be performed in many different ways, hence making it difficult to define a general description for each activity [13]. Classification models applied in activity recognition should therefore be able to deal with this situation. Given that the CBCE approach only considers the similarity between instances in the training and classification process, it is hypothesized that these approaches may have an advantage when dealing with this type of data. For instance-based classification methods there is no general definition required for each class (activity). A class label of a new instance is determined based on the class labels of some similar instances from the training set. Consequently, the most important concept is for representations of one class (activity) to be more similar with a specific representation than with the remaining alternatives. This can be satisfied, to a certain extent, by applying appropriate feature representations within the activity recognition problem.

4   Empirical Evaluation

For the purpose of this study a well known and publicly available data set[1] has been used. All information regarding the environment, sensors used and annotation applied during the data collection process can be found in [11]. Sensor data were collected over a period of 26 days in a 3- room apartment from a 26 year old male subject. Fourteen wireless sensors were installed in the apartment, each associated with one object: *'Microwave'*, *'Hall-Toilet door'*, *'Hall-Bathroom door'*, *'Cups cupboard'*, *'Fridge'*, *'Plates cupboard'*, *'Front door'*, *'Dishwasher'*, *'Toilet Flush'*, *'Freezer'*, *'Pans Cupboard'*, *'Washing machine'*, *'Groceries Cupboard'* and *'Hall-Bedroom door'*. Seven activities were observed throughout the duration of the experiments: *'Leave house'*, *'Use toilet'*, *'Take shower'*, *'Go to bed'*, *'Prepare breakfast'*, *'Prepare dinner'* and *'Get drink'*. In total there were 245 instances (activities) represented by 1,230 sensor events.

4.1   Data Pre-processing

In the activity recognition problem being considered instances are represented as a sequence of numbers/strings that may have different lengths. CBCE is an instance-based method that applies the Euclidean distance metric to calculate the distance between two instances. For this reason data to be used in the current study should be represented as vectors with the same dimension. The sensor recordings are initially converted into vectors of the same dimension. Consequently each instance (sequence of sensor labels) is represented by a 14-dimensional vector. Each dimension of the vector represents one sensor: $[S1,S2,S3,S4,S5,S6,S7,S8,S9,S10,S11,S12,S13]$. In the experiments, numeric and binary representations of the sensor recordings are considered. For the numeric representation the position in the vector is an indicator of how many times the sensor appears in the sequence. For the binary representation, the value for each position is either 1 or 0 subsequently indicating if the sensor appears or does not appear in the sequence, respectively. As an example the activity [*Hall-Bathroom door, Toilet Flush, Toilet Flush, Toilet Flush, Hall-Bathroom Door*] in the numeric system will be presented as: $[0,0,2,0,0,0,0,0,3,0,0,0,0,0]$. We can read from this vector that sensors S3 (*Hall-Bathroom door*) and S9 (*Toilet Flush*) appeared in the sequence 2 and 3 times, respectively. The same activity in the binary system will be presented as: $[0,0,1,0,0,0,0,0,1,0,0,0,0,0]$. From the binary vector we can read that sensors S3 and S9 appeared in the sequence although we do not have any information relating to their number of occurrences.

4.2   Implementation Details

The clustering process with CBCE is performed by the k-means[2] algorithm implemented in Weka[3] that uses the Euclidean distance metric[4]. For each clustering process

---

[1]   http://sites.google.com/site/tim0306/
[2]   weka.clusters.SimpleKMeans.

the number of clusters to be generated was randomly selected with the lower bound equal to the number of classes in the classification problem being considered and the upper bound equal to three times the number of classes. Any empty clusters generated in the training process were automatically removed. The upper bound was enforced in an effort to decrease the chance of very small or empty clusters being generated. Its value was selected based on an evaluation of the clustering technique on training data. In future work we aim to consider the number of clusters as a function of 3 variables, namely size of the training set, number of classes and number of features applied in the clustering process. With CBCE the number of features is randomly chosen as a value between 1 and the total number of features. For each generated cluster its centroid[5] is identified. Each categorical/numerical feature of the centroid is calculated as the mode/average of the values of the features stemming from all instances within the cluster. For the size of the ensemble $K=30$ was selected, following the evaluation of the model on the training set. The CBCE approach was compared with 3 single classification algorithms implemented in Weka. The classifiers considered were Naive Bayes[6] (NB), J48 Tree[7] (J48) and k Nearest Neighbour[8] (kNN).

5   Results and Discussion

For the experiments, a 5-fold cross-validation was performed. The accuracy was calculated as an average percentage of the correctly classified instances out of all instances in the testing set. In addition to accuracy, all methods were evaluated using F-measure [14]. Two main issues were investigated. The first issue was related to the two types of activity representation, namely binary and numeric, that were applied in the experiments. The second issue was related to the evaluation of CBCE in the activity recognition problem. Results obtained by the 5 methods for numeric and binary data are presented in Fig. 1a and 1b, respectively. It can be observed from Fig. 1a and 1b that kNN and CBCE obtained better results when applied with binary, rather than numeric data representation. J48 performed at the same level with both types of data representation, while for the NB classifier the difference was marginal. For binary data kNN and CBCE obtained the highest accuracies, while for numeric data they were both outperformed by NB. For numeric data, kNN and CBCE obtained significantly lower values of F-Measure which is an indication that they did not perform equally well in each class. kNN and CBCE are based on a similar approach, where the classification decision is made based on the distances measured between a new instance and instances from the training set. We can infer from this that for the two methods, whilst calculating the similarity between the two activities, it is more important to know which actions have been performed rather than how many times each actions took place. This can be explained by the fact that in the classification problem being considered the same activity can be represented by different combinations of

---

[3]   The Weka Data Mining Software: An Update SIGKDD Explorations, Volume 11, Issue 1.
[4]   weka.core.EuclideanDistance.
[5]   weka.clusters.SimpleKMeans.GetClustersCentroids.
[6]   weka.classifiers.bayes.NaiveBayes.
[7]   weka.classifiers.J48 –C 0.25 –M 2.
[8]   weka.classifiers.lazy.IBk –K 1 –W 0 –X –A.

actions. For example, while cooking dinner the fridge may be opened a different number of times. This may cause some problems while calculating the Euclidean distance between the same activities that have been performed in 2 different ways. It may also appear that two instances from the same class will be considered as being very distant.

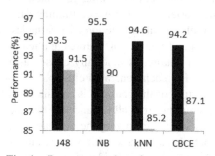 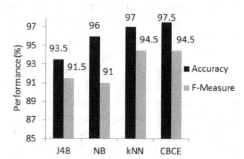

Fig. 1.a Percentage value of accuracy and F-Measure obtained for sensor data with numeric representation. J48 – J48 Tree, NB – Naïve Bayes, kNN–K Nearest Neighbour, CBCE-Cluster-Based Classifier Ensemble.

Fig. 1.b Percentage value of accuracy and F-Measure obtained for sensor data with binary representation. J48 – J48 Tree, NB – Naïve Bayes, kNN – K Nearest Neighbour, CBCE - Cluster-Based Classifier Ensemble.

Based on the results presented in Fig. 1.a and 1.b we can notice that the highest accuracy was obtained by CBCE (97.5%) and kNN (97%). Both of the methods outperformed NB (96%) and J48 (93.5%) in terms of accuracy and F-measure. This suggests that instance-based approaches are effective while applied in activity recognition problems. They not only obtained improved general accuracy, however, they also performed well in each class separately.

In addition to the accuracy it is, however, necessary to consider the computational cost of the methods. The training process of CBCE can be viewed as being complex as it requires clustering of the training set K different times. For large data sets this process may be time consuming. On the other hand, for a single kNN classifier no training is required. It should, however, be appreciated that following the training process, the classification of each new instance in the CBCE method is straight forward with limited computational cost. With the proposed approach a new instance needs to be compared with only a group of cluster centroids. For one base classifier the computational complexity can be estimated as $O(P{\times}l)$ where P and l represent number of clusters and features, respectively. For the kNN classifier, for number of instances in the training set equals N, the complexity can be estimated as $O(N{\times}l)$, which for large training data sets can be time consuming. We can therefore note that even though the CBCE approach requires a longer training process than kNN, it is, however, more efficient in terms of classification time. Once the ensemble is generated, classification of a new instance is a very simple task.

6   Conclusions

It can be concluded that instance-based methods are beneficial when applied in activity recognition problems compared to other classification techniques. Beside this, the experimental results demonstrate that instance-based classification methods perform better with binary rather than numeric representation of activities. This study provides a basis for further investigation into the application of ensemble methods in activity recognition within the application domain of smart homes. The new ensemble-based classification model was presented as being more accurate than a number of single classifiers. The study presented in the paper may be considered as early stage and further work is still intended. The first problem to be considered in the future work is an improved approach to selecting parameters for the model. It is presumed that appropriate selection of the number of clusters and the subset of features applied in the clustering process will improve the performance of the model.

References

1. Hong, X., Nugent, C.D., Mulvenna, M.D., McClean, S.I., Scotney, B.W., Devlin, S.: Evidential fusion of sensor data for activity recognition in smart homes. Pervasive Mobile Computing 5(3), 236–252 (2009)
2. Philipose, M., Fishkin, K., Perkowits, M., Patterson, D., Kautz, H., Hahnel, D.: Inferring activities from interactions with objects. IEEE Pervasive Computing Magazine 3(4), 50–57 (2004)
3. Rashidi, P., Cook, D., Holder, L., Schmitter-Edgecombe, M.: Discovering Activities to Recognize and Track in a Smart Environment. IEEE Trans. Knowl. Data Engineering 23(4), 527–539 (2011)
4. Tapia, E.M., Intille, S.S., Larson, K.: Activity Recognition in the Home Using Simple and Ubiquitous Sensors. In: Ferscha, A., Mattern, F. (eds.) PERVASIVE 2004. LNCS, vol. 3001, pp. 158–175. Springer, Heidelberg (2004)
5. Hasan, M., Rubaiyeat, H., Lee, Y., Lee, S.: A HMM for Activity Recognition. In: 10th International Conference Advanced Communication Technology, pp. 843–846 (2008)
6. Logan, B., Healey, J., Philipose, M., Tapia, E.M., Intille, S.S.: A long-term evaluation of sensing modalities for activity recognition. In: Krumm, J., Abowd, G.D., Seneviratne, A., Strang, T. (eds.) UbiComp 2007. LNCS, vol. 4717, pp. 483–500. Springer, Heidelberg (2007)
7. Yang, J.Y., Wang, J.S., Chen, Y.P.: Using acceleration measurements for activity recognition: An effective learning algorithm for constructing neural classifiers. Pattern Recognition Letters, 2213–2220 (2008)
8. Chen, L., Nugent, C.D., Wang, H.: A Knowledge-Driven Approach to Activity Recognition in Smart Homes. IEEE Transaction on Knowledge and Data Engineering 24(6), 961–974 (2012)
9. Jurek, A., Bi, Y., Wu, S., Nugent, C.D.: A survey of commonly used ensemble-based classification techniques. Cambridge University Press (in press, 2013)
10. Jurek, A., Bi, Y., Wu, S., Nugent, C.D.: A Cluster-Based Classifier Ensemble as an Alternative to the Nearest Neighbour Ensemble. In: 24th IEEE International Conference on Tools with Artificial Intelligence, pp. 1100–1105 (2012)
11. van Kasteren, T.: Activity Recognition for Health Monitoring Elderly using Temporal Probabilistic Models. UvA Universiteit van Amsterdam, Ph.D. thesis (2011)
12. Powers, D.: Evaluation: From Precision, Recall and F-Factor to ROC, Informedness, Markedness & Correlation. Machine Learning Technologies 2(1), 37–63 (2011)
13. Palmes, P., Pung, H.K., Gu, T., Xue, W., Chen, S.: Object relevance weight pattern mining for activity recognition and segmentation. Pervasive and Mobile Computing 6(1), 43–57 (2010)
14. Hoey, J., Plotz, T., Jackson, D., Monk, A., Pham, C., Olivier, P.: Rapid specification and automated generation of prompting systems to assist people with dementia. Pervasive and Mobile Computing 7(3), 299–318 (2011)

A Vision System for Intelligent Monitoring of Activities of Daily Living at Home

Alexandros Andre Chaaraoui, José Ramón Padilla-López,
Francisco Javier Ferrández-Pastor, Juan Manuel García-Chamizo,
Mario Nieto-Hidalgo, Vicente Romacho-Agud, and Francisco Flórez-Revuelta

Department of Computer Technology, University of Alicante,
P.O. Box 99, E-03080 Alicante, Spain
{alexandros,jpadilla,
fjferran,juanma,mnieto,vagud,florez}@dtic.ua.es

Abstract. Social progress and demographic changes favor increased life expectancy and the number of people in situations of dependency. As a consequence, the demand for support systems for personal autonomy is increasing. This article outlines the vision @ home project, whose goal is the development of vision-based services for monitoring and recognition of the activity carried out by individuals in the home. Incorporating vision devices in private settings is justified by its power to extract large amounts of data with low cost but must safeguard the privacy of individuals. The vision system we have designed incorporates a knowledge base containing information from the environment, parameters of different cameras used, human behavior modeling and recognition, and information about people and objects. By analyzing the scene, we infer its context, and provide a privacy filter which is able to return textual information, as well as synthetic and real images.

Keywords: behavior analysis, human action recognition, active aging, vision privacy.

1 Introduction

Video cameras are used mainly in video surveillance systems in order to guarantee security on the streets. They are used in outdoor environments and in public places but rarely within private environments mainly due to people worries about being continuously monitored and privacy violations. However, using video cameras in private spaces could suppose the born of novel applications in the field of ambient-assisted living (AAL) and particularly in health, home care and ageing in place. Building a smart environment like a smart home, sensitive to the user and his context and able of acting proactively to satisfy its inhabitants necessities, could impact the life of the elderly and disabled people living there, improving their quality of life and maintaining their independence.

In this environment, smart cameras can be used to analyze video streams targeting some incidents like people falling, shower accidents, thief intrusions, and so on.

C. Nugent, A. Coronato, and J. Bravo (Eds.): IWAAL 2013, LNCS 8277, pp. 96–99, 2013.
© Springer International Publishing Switzerland 2013

Whenever an incident is detected, the smart home could warn somebody (family member, care service, etc.) in order to get human confirmation and, above everything, to get assistance. Furthermore, it is required that these technologies guarantee privacy preservation of the inhabitants.

Regarding human behavior analysis, human action recognition constitutes the first level in which a semantic understanding of the human behavior can be obtained. Once motion has been detected in the scene, commonly a region of interest is obtained using background subtraction or human detection techniques [1]. In this sense, using human silhouettes as input, Bobick and Davis [2] proposed the motion history and energy images (MHI, MEI) in which respectively the age and the spatial location of pixel-wise motion is encoded. Other approaches rely on local information as key points and space-time interest points. Key point detectors have been extended to consider the temporal dimension [3]. These dense approaches present the advantage that they can be applied directly on the RGB image, without requiring necessarily a specific region of interest or background subtraction.

Recently, the launch of the Microsoft Kinect sensor made it possible to obtain depth information and marker-less human body pose estimation relatively accurately along with low cost and real-time performance. This is resulting in a large amount of work and related publications [4].

Regarding privacy, we consider it as the right of an individual to protect the information which he wants to keep private. Privacy is protected when there does not exist any association or mapping between sensitive information and person identity. Moreover, which information is considered sensitive depends on each individual.

Current research mainly focuses on redaction methods mixed with data hiding schemes. These rely on computer vision algorithms to determine privacy sensitive regions of the image that must be modified. There are a lot of types of image modification, such as private information removal leaving a black hole, use of blurring, pixelating and others commonly used image filters; or more robust methods like image encryption, face de-identification and image inpainting algorithms. However, for some of the described methods it has been demonstrated that they do not protect privacy [5], and others are not suitable for real time due to computational restrictions.

2   Human Action Recognition

Initially, we have established the type of human behaviors that are going to be considered as *actions* and aimed to be recognized during the execution of the *vision @ home* project. For this purpose, the state-of-the-art work has been considered in order to provide a common definition for the different levels of human behavior [6]. Two scales have been taken into account: 1) the amount of time during which the recognition needs to be performed, and 2) the degree of semantics that is involved in the comprehension of the behavior. In this sense, we define actions as human motion over a time frame from seconds to minutes in which simple human primitives as standing, sitting, walking and falling can be recognized.

- **Using RGB Images:** Relying on traditional RGB cameras, color images are processed by means of background subtraction techniques in order to obtain human silhouettes which serve as input to our method [7-9]. Nonetheless, these binary masks could also be obtained using other devices or approaches as infrared cameras or depth-based segmentation. Not the whole silhouette data is used, but only the contour points which encode the shape of the person and therefore its pose. We have proposed a low-dimensional feature in which a radial scheme is employed in order to spatially align the contour points [9]. Multiple cameras focusing the same field of view are also considered applying feature fusion techniques. Using the bag-of-key-poses model presented in [8], the most representative poses for each action class, the so called key poses, are learned. In contrast to traditional bag-of-words models, we do not perform recognition comparing the frequency of appearance of key poses, but learn the transition between key poses building sequences of key poses. These are learned substituting each pose with its nearest neighbor key pose, and therefore, changing the domain of the acquired data to the bag of key poses and filtering noise and sample-specific differences. Recognition is performed by means of sequence alignment using dynamic time warping (DTW). Experimentation performed on several publicly available datasets shows that not only state-of-the-art recognition results are obtained, but also suitability for real-time applications is given.
- **Using RGB-D Data:** With the marker-less body pose estimation which can be inferred using the data provided by a RGB-D sensor, fine-grained motions as gestures can also be detected. This constitutes a significant advantage over the former silhouette-based method. The body pose estimation is provided in the form of skeletal data. This kind of feature is studied in [10], where a genetic algorithm is proposed in order to select the optimal joints for human action recognition. Depending on the type of actions to recognize and on how these actions are performed by the actors, some joints may be redundant and others may even introduce noise and difficult the recognition. Therefore, and as shown in that contribution, the optimal feature subset can improve the final recognition and, at the same time, reduce its computational cost.

3   Privacy

In order to preserve privacy, we propose a level-based privacy protection scheme, where each level defines its own display model that determines how the captured scene is represented to the observer. Display models are responsible of rendering diminished representations of persons and objects appearing in the scene, and such task may involve removing from the scene all other people or activity that is not of interest for the observer. Using distinct display models we can provide several protection levels, from completely protected to unprotected, and observers with camera access can only view the information they are allowed to.

We have addressed the privacy of persons subject to monitoring through four different display formats of visual information: from the omission of the people, through virtual representations of the person in the scene, with or without the actual posture, to the accurate representation of the scene including the person.

4   Conclusions

In this paper, an outline of the research work and advances that have been made in the scope of the vision @ home project has been detailed. Using both traditional RGB images and the RGB-D data provided by the Microsoft Kinect device, several proposals have been made for human action recognition considering multiple views and achieving real-time performance. Depending on the persons in the scene, the activity that is being performed and the observer, different information about location, posture and scene analysis is provided.

References

1. Poppe, R.: A survey on vision-based human action recognition. Image Vision Comput. 28(6), 976–990 (2010)
2. Bobick, A.F., Davis, J.W.: The Recognition of Human Movement Using Temporal Templates. IEEE Transactions on Pattern Analysis and Machine Intelligence 23(3), 257–267 (2001)
3. Oikonomopoulos, A., Patras, I., Pantic, M.: Spatiotemporal salient points for visual recognition of human actions. IEEE Transactions on Systems, Man, and Cybernetics. Part B, Cybernetics: A Publication of the IEEE Systems, Man, and Cybernetics Society 36(3), 710–719 (2006)
4. Chen, L., Wei, H., Ferryman, J.M.: A Survey of Human Motion Analysis using Depth Imagery. Pattern Recognition Letters (February 2013)
5. Chen, D., Chang, Y., Yan, R., Yang, J.: Protecting personal identification in video. In: Senior, A. (ed.) Protecting Privacy in Video Surveillance, pp. 115–128. Springer, London (2009)
6. Chaaraoui, A.A., Climent-Pérez, P., Flórez-Revuelta, F.: A review on vision techniques applied to Human Behaviour Analysis for Ambient-Assisted Living. Expert Systems with Applications 39(12), 10873–10888 (2012)
7. Chaaraoui, A.A., Climent-Pérez, P., Flórez-Revuelta, F.: Silhouette-based Human Action Recognition using Sequences of Key Poses. Pattern Recognition Letters 34(15), 1799–1807 (2013), http://dx.doi.org/10.1016/j.patrec.2013.01.021
8. Chaaraoui, A.A., Climent-Pérez, P., Flórez-Revuelta, F.: An Efficient Approach for Multi-view Human Action Recognition Based on Bag-of-Key-Poses. In: Salah, A.A., Ruiz-del-Solar, J., Meriçli, Ç., Oudeyer, P.-Y. (eds.) HBU 2012. LNCS, vol. 7559, pp. 29–40. Springer, Heidelberg (2012)
9. Chaaraoui, A.A., Flórez-Revuelta, F.: Human Action Recognition Optimization Based on Evolutionary Feature Subset Selection. In: GECCO 2013: Proceedings of the 15th Annual Conference on Genetic and Evolutionary Computation (to appear, 2013)
10. Climent-Pérez, P., Chaaraoui, A., Padilla-López, J., Flórez-Revuelta, F.: Evolutionary joint selection to improve human action recognition with RGB-D devices. Expert Systems with Applications (2013) ISSN 0957-4174, http://dx.doi.org/10.1016/j.eswa.2013.08.009

Detecting Changes in Elderly's Mobility Using Inactivity Profiles

Rainer Planinc and Martin Kampel

Vienna University of Technology, Computer Vision Lab
Favoritenstrasse 9-11/183-2, A-1040 Vienna
{rainer.planinc,martin.kampel}@tuwien.ac.at

Abstract. Abnormal inactivity indicates situations, where elderly need assistance. Systems detecting the need for help models the amount of inactivity using inactivity profiles. Depending on the analysis of the profiles, events (e.g. falls) or long-term changes (decrease of mobility) are detected. Until now, inactivity profiles are only used to detect abnormal behavior on the short-term (e.g. fall, illness), but not on the long-term. Hence, this work introduces an approach to detect significant changes on mobility using long-term inactivity profiles, since these changes indicate enhanced or decreased mobility of elderly. Preliminary results are obtained by the analysis of the motion data of an elderly couple over the duration of 100 days and illustrates the feasibility of this approach.

Keywords: inactivity profiles, AAL, mobility, elderly.

1 Introduction

Staying in their own home as long as possible is a great challenge for elderly, since risks of living on their own home rise. The risk of falling is reported to be a major risk for elderly since it might take hours until they are found and help is provided [1]. However, not only falls are a great risk for elderly, but also the decrease of mobility results in a lower quality of life [2]. Studies either focus on detecting events directly (e.g. falls [3–5]) or detecting events indirectly by detecting abnormal inactivity (e.g. [6–8]). The latter offer the advantage to detect different critical circumstances at the same time (e.g. falls, illness) but only analyze short-term behavior (i.e. less than 24 hours). Hence, the aim of this paper is the detection of mobility changes of elderly by introducing long-term analysis of inactivity profiles (i.e. over the duration of several months). Detecting a decrease of mobility already at an early stage ensures that countermeasures can be taken to prevent the further decrease of mobility. Moreover, an increase of mobility indicates a more active and thus healthy lifestyle.

Detection of falls using inactivity zones is introduced by Nait-Charif & McKenna [8]. The scene is modeled using entry, exit and inactivity zones. Inactivity zones are areas, where almost no activity is detected (e.g. bed). If a person is located outside a pre-defined inactivity zone and no activity is detected over a longer period of time, an alarm is raised. This information is then used to detect

C. Nugent, A. Coronato, and J. Bravo (Eds.): IWAAL 2013, LNCS 8277, pp. 100–103, 2013.

falls, since falls are defined as unusual inactivity occuring outside of inactivity zones.

Cuddihy et al. [6] and Floeck & Litz [7] introduced methods to detect abnormal long inactivity based on motion and door sensors. Both calculate inactivity profiles, i.e. the duration of inactivity at a specific time of the day is measured and a standard behavior is trained. In the work of Floeck & Litz [7], a day is divided into i timeslots, the integral of the inactivity of each timeslot is calculated and stored as a vector. The vector is then compared to a pre-trained reference vector and deviations raise alarms. This comparison is calculated once a day, since the data of the whole day is taken into consideration. In contrast, Cuddihy et al. [6] calculates an alert line from the training data and compare each timeslot to this alert line individually. If the inactivity of a specific timeslot is above the alert line, an alarm is raised immediately.

The rest of this work is structured as follows: Section 2 introduces the proposed approach to detect long-term behavioral changes in mobility using inactivity profiles, whereas Section 3 presents preliminary results of our work. Finally, a conclusion is drawn in Section 4.

2   Methodology

In contrast to the state-of-the-art, this work proposes the anlysis of changes in the long-term behavior in order to detect a change of mobility. The algorithm of Cuddihy et al. [6] detects an unusual inactivity if the inactivity level is above the trained alert line. Hence, short-term changes (i.e. in the range of hours) are detected (e.g. illness, fall). The alert line is calculated using a rolling window, i.e. the last 45 days are considered during the calculation of the alert line. This ensures that the algorithm is able to adopt to changes and thus reduces the number of false alarms. However, due to the adoption, a slow change of activity (e.g. over the course of a year) can not be detected since the algorithm is adopted on the basis of the rolling window. Due to this, the approach introduced in this paper compares alert lines (e.g. on a monthly basis) in order to be able to extract a general trend and detects significant changes of mobility over the course of a year.

The proposed method uses the calculation of an alert line described in [6], resulting in an inactivity threshold $ALERT_i$ for every time interval i. The interval is set to one minute, resulting in 1440 intervals per day. Alert lines are stored at regular intervals (e.g. one alert line per month), resulting in t different alert lines. The arithmetic average μ and standard deviation σ of all alert lines t are calculated for each interval i. During the training phase, all alert lines are incorporated to the calculation of the average alert line. After the training phase (e.g. three months), the deviation of the alert line to be added is calculated using the following rule: if the deviation of more than 25% (i.e. six hours) of the alert line intervals is within the range of $\mu \pm 2\sigma$, the average alert line is updated. If more than 25% of the alert line intervals are outside the range of $\mu \pm 2\sigma$, a significant change in long-term mobility is detected. Depending on the direction of

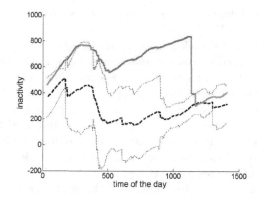

Fig. 1. Deviation of alert line indicating higher inactivity and hence decreased mobility

the change (i.e. higher or lower inactivity compared to the reference alert line), a reduction resp. increase of mobility is reported.

An example of a deviation is shown in Figure 1: the trained average alert line is shown as thick dashed line, whereas the other dashed lines indicate the range of $\mu \pm 2\sigma$. The alert line to be tested is visualized as green solid line and time intervals outside the range of $\mu \pm 2\sigma$ are visualized as magenta parts of the alert line. In this case it can be also visually verified that more than 25% of the alert line are outside the boundary and hence, a deviation in comparison to the "normal" mobility is detected. Since the alert line indicates a higher inactivity, a reduction of mobility is detected.

3   Results

For the preliminary evaluation the activity data of an elderly couple over the duration of 100 days is analyzed. The couple is 72 resp. 66 years old and in a good health condition, i.e. no problems with mobility or balance were reported. Moreover, activities of daily living can be performed without additional help, hence both are able to live independently. The Kinect was used as motion sensor and placed in the living room of the couple, monitoring the dining table and the surrounding area. This area was choosen since the couple performs regular food intake at the dining table and thus results in regular patterns. Since only a small, but important and regularly visited area of the flat was monitored, no additional devices (e.g. sensors, accelerometers) were used. There was no direct sunlight reported in this area, hence accurate depth data can be obtained. In order to evaluate results, alert lines based on 25 days intervals are generated, resulting in four long-term alert lines. For evaluation the leave-one-out cross-validation method is used, hence three alert lines are used for training whereas the fourth alert line is tested. The algorithm detected one significant decrease of mobility within the test period, depicted in Figure 1, where 64.7% of intervals are outside the specified range. During this intervall, the couple was on a journey, thus resulting in an increased inactivity. However, all three other alert lines are within the specified range, since only 21.1%, 3.7% and 1% of the time intervals are outside the range and thus considered to be outliers or only minor changes in mobility.

4 Conclusion

Analyzing inactivity profiles on the long-term allows to detect changes in mobility. Since these changes are more likely to be a decrease than an increase of mobility, countermeasures to enhance the mobility can be taken already at an early stage and thus resulting in an enhanced quality of life of elderly. The approach introduced in this paper is able to detect changes in mobility by comparing the inactivity profile with a reference profile and detects deviations automatically. Preliminary results are promising and a decrease of mobility of an elderly couple was detected correctly. However, future work will deal with an more extensive evaluation and validation on a larger dataset.

Acknowledgments. This work is supported by the European Union under grant AAL 2010-3-020. The authors want to thank the whole fearless project team, since techniques and ideas of many researchers involved are used.

References

1. Wild, D., Nayak, U.S., Isaacs, B.: How dangerous are falls in old people at home? British Medical Journal (Clinical Research Ed.) 282(6260), 266–268 (1981)
2. Farquhar, M.: Elderly people's definitions of quality of life. Social Science & Medicine 41(10), 1439–1446 (1995)
3. Anderson, D., Luke, R.H., Keller, J.M., Skubic, M., Rantz, M., Aud, M.: Linguistic Summarization of Video for Fall Detection Using Voxel Person and Fuzzy Logic. Computer Vision and Image Understanding 113(1), 80–89 (2009)
4. Mastorakis, G., Makris, D.: Fall detection system using Kinects infrared sensor. Journal of Real-Time Image Processing (March 2012)
5. Rougier, C., Meunier, J., St-Arnaud, A., Rousseau, J.: Fall Detection from Human Shape and Motion History Using Video Surveillance. In: Advanced Information Networking and Applications Workshops, pp. 875–880. IEEE, Niagara Falls (2007)
6. Cuddihy, P., Weisenberg, J., Graichen, C., Ganesh, M.: Algorithm to automatically detect abnormally long periods of inactivity in a home. In: Proc. of the International Workshop on Systems and Networking Support for Healthcare and Assisted Living Environments HealthNet 2007, pp. 89–94. ACM, NY (2007)
7. Floeck, M., Litz, L.: Activity- and Inactivity-Based Approaches to Analyze an Assisted Living Environment. In: Second International Conference on Emerging Security Information, Systems and Technologies, pp. 311–316 (2008)
8. Nait-Charif, H., McKenna, S.: Activity summarisation and fall detection in a supportive home environment. In: Proc. of the International Conference on Pattern Recognition (ICPR), vol. 4, pp. 323–326. IEEE (2004)

An Integral Medicine Taking Solution
for Mild and Moderate Alzheimer Patients

Gabriel Urzaiz[1], Eric Murillo[1], Sergio Arjona[1], Ramon Hervas[2], Jesus Fontecha[2],
and José Bravo[2]

[1] Universidad Anahuac Mayab, Merida, Yucatan, Mexico
{gabriel.urzaiz,eric.murillo,sergio.arjona}@anahuac.mx
[2] Universidad de Castilla-La Mancha, Ciudad Real, Spain
{ramon.hlucas,jesus.fontecha,jose.bravo}@uclm.es

Abstract. A comprehensive solution is proposed to enhance adherence for the mild and moderate Alzheimer patients, involving not only the patient but also other participants, such as the nurse and/or relative, the drugstore, the physician and the hospital. The solution includes the development of an automatic medication dispenser and the corresponding software applications. In this article a general schema of the solution is presented, and a brief description of the first hardware and software prototypes is also included.

Keywords: adherence, compliance, concordance, medicine-taking, dispenser.

1 Introduction

Dementia is a disease characterized by loss of cognitive abilities inducing impairment in normal daily activities [1, 2]. Among the disturbances that cause dementia, Alzheimer's disease (AD) is the most common neurodegenerative disorder and it is defined by clinical and pathological criteria. For example, it displays neurodegenerative profile, presence of extracellular amyloid plaques, and intraneuronal neurofibrillary tangles causing memory loss [3]. From the clinical perspective, AD is characterized by memory loss and decrease in other cognitive abilities [4-7].

Aging is the main risk factor for AD, with the prevalence doubling every 5 years after the age of 65 [8]. According to the National Institute on Aging, it has been estimated that as many as 5.1 million Americans have AD [9]. The prevalence of AD has been is estimated to grow to nearly 9 million individuals in America by 2050. The worldwide prevalence of dementia is estimated to be 35.6 million in 2010, with the number exceeding 65 million in 2030 and 115 million in 2050, making it a pressing global health concern [10]. According to the National Institute on Aging, AD is divided into 3 stages:

1. Mild AD: This stage is characterized by an initial memory loss. Problems such as getting lost, trouble handling money and paying bills, repeating questions, poor judgment, and changes in mood and personality, are present in this initial phase.

C. Nugent, A. Coronato, and J. Bravo (Eds.): IWAAL 2013, LNCS 8277, pp. 104–111, 2013.

2. Moderate AD: In this stage, brain damage is presented in areas that control language, reasoning, sensory processing, and cognitive functions. Memory loss and confusion grow worse. Patients display problems to recognize family or friends. They also show significant problems to learn new tasks. Additionally, hallucinations, delusions, and paranoia, are also present in this second phase.
3. Severe AD: In this last stage, brain areas display significant neurodegenerative processes and brain tissue has shrunk significantly. In the final stage of this disease, patients lose the ability to respond to their environment, to carry on a conversation and, eventually, to control movement. Also, patients with AD at severe stage need help with much of their daily personal care, including eating or using the toilet. Thus, patients diagnosed with severe AD display inability to communicate and are completely dependent on others for their care.

Thus, the increase in the number of patients with AD could represent an unfavorable condition from various aspects: from the social, economic, and those related to public health. With this scenario, it is important to generate new approaches to manage certain conditions arising from AD, such the daily life of patients.

Some of the authors of this article have previous work on Alzheimer's disease [11-12]. In this article, we propose a comprehensive solution to address the need for assistance to a patient with mild or moderate AD for taking medication, as well as his/her supervision at distance. The solution includes the development of an automatic medication dispenser and the corresponding software applications. In addition, it will represent a decisive response as to the lack of technological innovation and transfers its value to society, specifically aimed to a segment of the adult population of Alzheimer disease in early stages.

2   Revision

Patients with AD report cognitive impairment, memory deficits and neurodegenerative process. This condition, in advanced phases of the disease, represents a challenge for patients to remember the ingestion of the medications.

There are three terms that are used to describe patient's behavior with regards to the prescriber's recommendations. These terms are compliance, adherence and concordance, Although they are commonly used interchangeably, they have slightly different meanings. Horne et al [13] recommend adherence as the term of choice to describe patients' medicine taking behavior. It is defined as the extent in which the patient's behavior matches agreed recommendations from the prescriber, emphasizing that the patient is free to decide whether to adhere to the doctor's recommendations and that failure to do so should not be a reason to blame the patient.

Automation is a concept that promotes drug-dispensing system in hospitals. Such systems have advantages for the patient, for example, favor adherence and use of the drug, and also prevent uncomfortable hospital transfers, thus reducing waiting times in consultation.

There are several dispensers [14], such as the Philips Medication Dispensing Service Works [15], among many others. The Philips dispenser (which price is about

US$ 895.00) loads drugs placed in small containers which are fed into the dispenser. The dispenser is programmed according to the needs of the patient. The patient presses a button when he or she hears the reminder alarm. The dispenser delivers the medicine that has been already loaded. The dispenser is connected to the telephone line of the patient; thus, in case the patient misses taking the medicine, then the family is contacted.

There are also interesting proposals in the scientific community, for example, Jara et. al. [16] designed a system based on the Internet of Things (IoT) for the drug identification and the monitoring of medication. Shafti et. al. [17] proposed a Personal Ambient Intelligent Reminder (PAIR) that is intended to assist subjects with cognitive disabilities (CD). There are also smartphone applications, such as PEAT [18] which are specifically designed for people with loss or reduction of cognitive abilities. Coronato and De Pietro [19] present an approach for the detection of abnormal behaviors of cognitive impaired people, based on the specification and runtime verification of correctness properties.

3   Motivation

While the market offers different types of medical devices, there are further areas that need to be considered as part of the solution. Despite the existence of medical dispensers, further problems related with missing the prescription are still present. According to the literature, approximately 1 in 10 older adult admissions to hospitals are the result of misuse of drugs [20]. This implies that patients with AD, are at risk of not taking medications properly, causing serious consequences, such as increased discomfort, even death.

Foreman et al [21] reported that subjects adopt a program taking medication reminder using cell phone text messages, show greater adherence to treatment compared with subjects who did not use such a reminder system. So, it can be hypothetized that a medication reminder system that is digitally linked to the patient-doctor-nurse-family will provide a direct response and it will determine the improvement of the quality of life of patients with AD.

The main aim of this proposal is to develop a comprehensive solution to enhance adherence for the mild and moderate AD patients. Our solution will facilitate to the patients with AD at state 1 (mild AD) and state 2 (moderate AD) a reliable device and a comprehensive solution to provide a reminder to take medications in a timely manner. It is very important to say that the solution is designed to assist and facilitate the medication-taking process, and it is not intended to assume the responsibilities of the nurse, the relatives, the physician or anyone else involved in the process.

Our proposal covers different aspects such as the location of the subject within the home and, depending on the subject's physical location, an alarm will be played as a reminder for the patient for medication. Since AD patients present diminution in cognitive capabilities, the medication dispenser uses several alarm types to ensure the effectiveness of the reminder (flashing light, sound and vibration to call attention, and a marquee to display a message to remind the needed action).

4   Solution

The proposed solution (Fig. 1) involves not only the medication dispenser, but also the integration of all participants on a single platform, so that they can interact and collaborate for the benefit of medication-taking process of the AD patient.

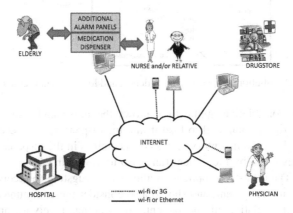

Fig. 1. The proposed solution: participants and wide area interconnection

The technological solution includes the design and development of hardware and software components, which serve as the interaction elements of each of the participants (interfaces and specific applications in each of the devices).

The hardware components are: the medication dispenser, and the additional alarm panels. The software components are: the application for nurse and/or relative, the application for drugstore, the application for the physician, and the application for the hospital.

The medication dispenser (DAME) is an automatic device which offers to the patient an easy and effective way to take his or her medicines. The nickname comes from the Spanish phrase "Dispensador Automático de MEdicamentos", which may be literally translated to English as "automatic medication dispenser".

The dispenser interface mainly consists of a series of gates on which the drugs are placed to be delivered to the patient. It also includes an alarm board to indicate and remind the patient when it's time to take some drug.

The dispenser should be placed in a strategic location of the house (e.g. the living & dining room, which is probably one of the places where the patient spends more time) and additional motion detection sensors and alarm panels should be installed in the remainder rooms (Fig. 2), to be received even when the patient is away from the dispenser. All alarm panels will be connected to the dispenser by using a short-distance wireless technology, such as Bluetooth or Xbee. The medication dispenser is also connected to a PC which serves as a geteway to the Internet, and it also has an NFC interface to connect to the nurse and/or relative smartphone application.

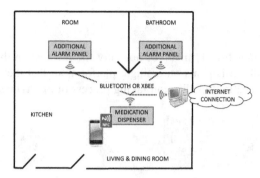

Fig. 2. Distribution of spaces in a residence, and local area interconnection

The nurse and/or relative application allows the nurse and / or the relative to capture the prescription plan and to load it into the dispenser, to receive and manage the information about the inventory (stock) of medicines in the dispenser, and to keep track of the drugs taken by the patient (and also to advise in case of a drug that was not taken, etc.). The drugstore application allows the drugstore to receive drug orders which were automatically sent, and should also consider the communication with the nurse and / or the relative of the patient, for sending, receiving and paying for medicine. The platform will enable the physician for to have access to information regarding patient therapeutic adherence. Additionally it will improve efficiency in certain tasks such as more adequate appointment scheduling for patients requiring direct supervision. Finally, the system will allow the doctor to have direct contact with both the nurse and the relative in case of unattended alarms.

One objective in the development of DAME, is to be used by health systems in the country (public and private). So that, once the dispenser is installed at subject's home, the doctor from his office is able to directly access real-time information on dosages, failure in the supply of drugs, alarms triggered by a failure to take medication, etc. This device will streamline the resources in hospitals, due to the fact that having real-time information regarding abnormality in the medicine-taking process, the physician may give notice to relatives without leaving his or her hospital responsibilities.

5   First Prototype Implementation

Preliminary prototypes of the medication dispenser and the additional alarm panels are now been implemented, and the first version of the application for the nurse and/or the relative is also being developed.

The medication dispenser prototype includes a gate array to load the different drugs, and a front panel with a single gate to deliver them to the patient. We used an Arduino to implement the electronic logic, and Xbee modules to communicate with the additional alarm modules and with a PC serving as a gateway to the Internet.

The dispenser consists of four main components: delivery, filling, distribution, and communications. The delivery component is the interface that will interact with the patient. Its main function is to easily deliver the drugs that correspond at each time.

The delivery component comprises three elements: The delivery gate, on which the drugs are placed to be delivered to the patient; the alarm board, which includes a visual alarm, an audible alarm and a digital marquee to display the message "TAKE MEDICINE"; and a camera, which generates an image of the moment in which the patient takes medication. When it's time to take medication the alarm panel at the dispenser is activated, and the delivery gate is opened automatically containing the appropriate medicines. The delivery gate has a sensor to notify if the medication has been taken or not. It automatically takes a photo at the time in which the drug is being taken to ensure that the patient takes his medicine. If the drug has not been removed, the alarm will remain activated at predetermined intervals until the patient removes the medicine. In case it was not removed after a predetermined time, a message is automatically sent to the nurse and / or relative to warn that the patient did not take a certain drug.

The filling component is the element where medications are placed originally. There is a compartment for each of the different medications that the doctor prescribes. Each compartment has a numerical indicator related to the number of units (tablets, lozenges, etc.) in existence, so that it can easily be known in advance when to fill certain compartment. At the time in which the existence of drugs in a compartment reaches a predetermined threshold, an automatic message is sent to the drugstore (asking to send to the address the requested drug) and the nurse and / or relative (to receive the drug and place it in the corresponding compartment in the dispenser).

The distribution component is the element responsible for distributing drugs, taking them from magazines where they were originally filled, separating and accommodating them into the delivery compartment as appropriate in accordance with the schedules and instructions prescribed by the doctor.

The communications component includes an Xbee connection to communicate with the PC that serves as a gateway to the Internet and with the additional alarm panels that will be installed at different rooms of the house, and it also includes an NFC interface to provide an easy way to interact with it. In previous works we used NFC and it has proven to be a good alternative for nurse interaction [22] and as a part of the prescription process [23].

The first piece of software that is being developed is the nurse and/or relative application. The application is based on HTML5 and will be available for Android-based smartphones and tablets, and for PC. The application includes two main components. The first part is dedicated to capture the prescription plan and to load it into the dispenser, and the second component is used to receive and organize the information that comes from the dispenser. This second component is also used to send specific commands to be executed at the dispenser (reset counters, manage alarms, etc.).

6   Conclusion and Work in Progress

A comprehensive solution is proposed to collaborate for the benefit of medication-taking process of patients with Alzheimer disease in mild or moderate state.

A first hardware prototype is being built, including the medication dispenser and the additional alarm panels, and a first application for the nurse and/or relative is also being developed in order to test interaction through the platform.

Future work includes the development of an enhanced dispenser prototype, the development of the applications for all the other participants, and testing to determine the adherence improvement.

Acknowledgment. We recognize and thank David Herrera and Fernando Schlitter for their contribution on the construction of the first hardware and software prototype.

References

1. Cipriani, G., Vedovello, M., Ulivi, M., Nuti, A., Lucetti, C.: Repetitive and Stereotypic Phenomena and Dementia. Am. J. Alzheimers Dis. Other Demen. (in press, 2013)
2. Galasko, D.: The diagnostic evaluation of a patient with dementia. Continuum (Minneap Minn) 19(2 Dementia), 397–410 (2013), doi:10.1212/01.CON.0000429176.37224.58
3. Serý, O., Povová, J., Míšek, I., Pešák, L., Janout, V.: Molecular mechanisms of neuropathological changes in Alzheimer's disease: a review. Folia Neuropathol. 51, 1–9 (2013)
4. Jicha, G.A., Carr, S.A.: Conceptual evolution in Alzheimer's disease: implications for understanding the clinical phenotype of progressive neurodegenerative disease. J. Alzheimers Dis. 19, 253–272 (2010), doi:10.3233/JAD-2010-1237
5. Stern, C., Munn, Z.: Cognitive leisure activities and their role in preventing dementia: a systematic review. Int. J. Evid. Based Healthc. 8, 2–17 (2010), doi:10.1111/j.1744-1609.2010.00150.x
6. Thalhauser, C.J., Komarova, N.L.: Alzheimer's disease: rapid and slow progression. J. R. Soc. Interface 9, 119–126 (2012), doi:10.1098/rsif.2011.0134
7. Williams, J.W., Plassman, B.L., Burke, J., Benjamin, S.: Preventing Alzheimer's disease and cognitive decline. Evid. Rep. Technol. Assess. (Full Rep.) 193, 1–727 (2010)
8. Brookmeyer, R., Gray, S., Kawas, C.: Projections of Alzheimer's disease in the United States and the public health impact of delaying disease onset. Am. J. Public Health 88, 1337–1342 (1998)
9. National Institute on Aging. Alzheimer's Disease Fact Sheet, http://www.nia.nih.gov/alzheimers/publication/ alzheimers-disease-fact-sheet (accessed on May 31, 2013)
10. Alzheimer's Disease International. World Alzheimer Report 2009 (2009), http://www.alz.co.uk/research/files/World%20Alzheimer%20Report. pdf (accessed on September 30, 2009)
11. Bravo, J., López-de-Ipiña, D., Fuentes, C., Hervás, R., Peña, R., Vergara, M., Casero, G.: Enabling NFC Technology for Supporting Chronic Diseases: A Proposal for Alzheimer Caregivers. In: Aarts, E., Crowley, J.L., de Ruyter, B., Gerhäuser, H., Pflaum, A., Schmidt, J., Wichert, R. (eds.) AmI 2008. LNCS, vol. 5355, pp. 109–125. Springer, Heidelberg (2008)
12. Bravo, J., Hervás, R., Gallego, R., Casero, G., Vergara, M., Carmona, T., Fuentes, C., Nava, S.W., Chavira, G., Villarreal, V.: Identification Technologies to Support Alzheimer Contexts. In: ACM International Workshop on Ambient Assistive Technologies for Intelligent Healthcare Services (AASTIH 2008) in 1st International Conference on PErvasive Technologies Related to Assistive Environments (PETRA 2008), Athens, Greece (July 2008)

13. Horne, R., Weinman, J., Barber, N., Elliot, R., Morgan, M., Cribb, A.: Concordance, adherence and compliance in medicine taking. NCCSDO, London (2005)
14. e-pill Medication Reminders, http://www.epill.com/ (accessed on June 7, 2013)
15. Philips Medication Dispenser, http://www.epill.com/philipsmd.html; http://www.managemypills.com/content/ (accessed on May 31, 2013)
16. Jara, A.J., Zamora, M.A., Skarmeta, F.A.: Drug identification and interaction checker based on IoT to minimize adverse drug reactions and improve drug compliance. Personal and Ubiquitous Computing, 1–13 (2012), doi:10.1007/s00779-012-0622-2
17. Shafti, L.S., Haya, P.A., García-Herranz, M., Alamán, X.: Personal Ambient Intelligent Reminder for People with Cognitive Disabilities. In: Bravo, J., Hervás, R., Rodríguez, M. (eds.) IWAAL 2012. LNCS, vol. 7657, pp. 383–390. Springer, Heidelberg (2012)
18. Meet PEAT: A life-changing Android app for people with cognitive challenges, http://brainid.com/ (accessed on June 4, 2013)
19. Coronato, A., De Pietro, G.: Situation awareness in applications of ambient assisted living for cognitive impaired people. Mobile Networks and Applications 18(3), 444–453 (2012)
20. Krähenbühl-Melcher, A., Schlienger, R., Lampert, M., Haschke, M., Drewe, J., Krähenbühl, S.: Drug-related problems in hospitals: a review of the recent literature. Drug Saf. 30, 379–407 (2007)
21. Foreman, K.F., Stockl, K.M., Le, L.B., Fisk, E., Shah, S.M., Lew, H.C., Solow, B.K., Curtis, B.S.: Impact of a text messaging pilot program on patient medication adherence. Clin. Ther. 34, 1084–1091 (2012), doi:10.1016/j.clinthera.2012.04.007
22. Fontecha, J., Hervás, R., Villarreal, V., Bravo, J.: An NFC Approach for Nursing Care Training. In: 3rd International Workshop on Near Field Communication, Hagenberg, Austria, February 22-23 (2011)
23. Vergara, M., Díaz-Hellín, P., Fontecha, J., Hervás, R., Sánchez-Barba, C., Fuentes, C., Bravo, J.: Mobile prescription: An NFC-based proposal for AAL. In: Proceedings of the 2nd International Workshop on Near Field Communication, Monaco, April 20-22, pp. 27–32 (2010)

Human Facial Expression Recognition Using Wavelet Transform and Hidden Markov Model

Muhammad Hameed Siddiqi and Sungyoung Lee*

Department of Computer Engineering, Kyung Hee University
(Global Campus), Suwon, Rep. of Korea
{siddiqi,sylee}@oslab.khu.ac.kr

Abstract. The accuracy of the Facial Expression Recognition (FER) system is completely reliant on the extraction of the informative features. In this work, a new feature extraction method is proposed that has the capability to extract the most prominent features from the human face. The proposed technique has been tested and validated in order to achieve the best accuracy for FER systems. There are some regions in the face that have much contribution in achieving the best accuracy. Therefore, in this work, the human face is divided into number of regions and in each region the movement of pixels have been traced. For this purpose, one of the wavelet families named symlet wavelet is used and individual facial frame is decomposed up to 2 levels. In each decomposition level, the distances between the pixels is found by using the distance formula and by this way some of the informative coefficients are extracted and hence the feature vector has been created. Moreover, the dimension of the feature space is reduced by employing a well-known statistical technique such as Linear Discriminant Analysis (LDA). Finally, Hidden Markov Model (HMM) is exploited for training and testing the system in order to label the expressions. The proposed FER system has been tested and validated on Cohn-Kanade dataset. The resulting recognition accuracy of 94% illustrates the success of employing the proposed technique for FER.

Keywords: Facial Expression Recognition, Wavelet Transform, LDA, HMM.

1 Introduction

Facial expression recognition (FER) plays a significant role in daily life communication. In daily life, various types of communication are utilized for human-to-human interactions: for instance, verbal and non-verbal communication, mental states, and physiological activities [6]. Among these, verbal communication (such

* This research was supported by the MSIP (Ministry of Science, ICT & Future Planning), Korea, under the ITRC (Information Technology Research Center) support program supervised by the NIPA (National IT Industry Promotion Agency) (NIPA-2013-(H0301-13-2001)).

C. Nugent, A. Coronato, and J. Bravo (Eds.): IWAAL 2013, LNCS 8277, pp. 112–119, 2013.

as speech) and non-verbal communication (such as facial expressions) [14] are most often employed. According to [14], during a face-to-face communication, the feelings of a person (such as like or dislike) depend just 7% on the spoken words, 38% on voice intonation, and an incredible 55% on facial expressions.

Generally, FER system consists of three basic modules: preprocessing, feature extraction and recognition. So far, there lots of works have been done for preprocessing including automatic face detection and for recognition modules. Most of the facial features are very sensitive regarding to noise and illumination and also there is very slight change in the facial pixels intensity, however, very limited work can be found for feature extraction in the literature.

Some of the previous works including [9, 12, 13] employed a well-known statistical technique like Principal Component Analysis (PCA) for facial feature extraction. However, PCA focuses only the global features and moreover computational wise PCA is much expensive [7]. In order to achieve high recognition rate, local facial features are very important, Therefore, to solve the problem of PCA, another higher-order statistical method named Independent Component Analysis (ICA) has been exploited by [1] and [4], which has capability to extract the informative local features from the face. However, if a huge amount of data is exploited as an input, ICA does not has the capability to handle these inputs and might lose informative features which we want.

Therefore, the authors of [3, 5, 11, 15] proposed Local Feature Analysis (LFA) and Local Non-negative Matrix Factorization (LNMF) in order to solve the limitations of statistical methods and to extract informative local facial features from the human face. However, LFA does not extract the local features when there are local distortion and partial occlusion in the pixels located in non-salient areas [10]. Similarly, one of the limitations of LNMF is that it does not assure the significant facial features in the localized area. Moreover, some time LNMF reduces the performance of FER systems because it has no ability to discriminate the features of cheek, forehead and jaw like areas [10].

The objective of this paper is to propose a new feature extraction technique based wavelet transform (especially symlet wavelet family). In this method, the human face is divided into number of regions and in each region the distance between the two pixels has been calculated by employing the distance formula. After that the average distance of each region is calculated and by this way the feature vector is calculated. In the second step of this method, the dimension of the feature space is reduced by exploiting a well-known linear classifier named Linear Discriminant Analysis (LDA), and finally, each expression is labeled by employing a well-known classifier like Hidden Markov Model (HMM).

We already described some related work about this field. The rest of the paper is organized as follows. Section 2 delivers an overview of the proposed feature extraction technique. Section 3 provides some experimental results along with some discussion on the results and a comparison with some of the widely used statistical feature extraction methods. Finally, the paper will be concluded after some future direction in Section 4.

2   Material and Method

2.1   Feature Extraction Using Wavelet Transform

Feature extraction deals with getting the distinguishable features from each facial expression shape and quantizing it as a discrete symbol.

In this stage, the decomposition process has been applied using symlet wavelet, for which the facial frames were in grey scale. The wavelet decomposition could be interpreted as signal decomposition in a set of independent feature vector. Each vector consists of sub-vectors like

$$V_0^{2D} = V_0^{2D-1}, V_0^{2D-2}, V_0^{2D-3}, \ldots\ldots, V_0^{2D-n} \tag{1}$$

where V represents the 2D feature vector. If we have 2D frame X it breaks up into orthogonal sub images corresponding to different visualization. The following equation shows one level of decomposition.

$$X = A_1 + D_1 \tag{2}$$

where X indicates the decomposed image and A_1 and D_1 are called approximation and detail coefficient vectors. If a facial frame is decomposed up to multiple levels, the Eq. 2 can then be written as

$$X = A_j + D_j + D_{j-1} + D_{j-2} + \ldots + D_2 + D_1 \tag{3}$$

where j represents the level of decomposition, and A and D represent the approximation and detail coefficients respectively. The detail coefficients mostly consist of noise, so for feature extraction only the approximation coefficients are used. In the proposed algorithm, each facial frame is decomposed up to two levels, i.e., the value of $j = 2$, because by exceeding the value of $j = 2$, the facial frame looses significant information, due to which the informative coefficients cannot be detected properly, which may cause misclassification. The detail coefficients further consist of three sub-coefficients, so the Eq. 3 can be written as

$$
\begin{aligned}
X &= A_2 + D_2 + D_1 \\
&= A_2 + [(D_h)_2 + (D_v)_2 + (D_d)_2] \\
&\quad + \quad [(D_h)_1 + (D_v)_1 + (D_d)_1]
\end{aligned}
\tag{4}
$$

where D_h, D_v and D_d are known as horizontal, vertical and diagonal coefficients respectively. It means that all the coefficients are connected with each other like a chain. Note that at each decomposition step, approximation and detail coefficient vectors are obtained by passing the signal through a low-pass filter and high-pass filter respectively.

In each decomposition level, the distance between the pixels is found by using the distance formula and by this way some of the informative coefficients are extracted and hence the feature vector has been created.

$$Dist = \sqrt{(x_2 - x_1)^2 + (y_2 - y_1)^2} \tag{5}$$

where (x_1, y_1) and (x_2, y_2) are the location of the two pixels respectively.

In a specified time window and frequency bandwith wavelet transform, the frequency is guesstimated. The signal (i.e., facial frame) is analyzed by using the wavelet transform [17].

$$C\left(a_i, b_j\right) = \frac{1}{\sqrt{a_i}} \int\limits_{-\infty}^{\infty} y\left(t\right) \Psi_{f.e}^* \left(\frac{t - b_j}{a_i}\right) dt \tag{6}$$

where a_i is the scale of the wavelet between lower frequency and upper frequency bounds to get high decision for frequency estimation, and b_j is the position of the wavelet from the start and end of the time window with the spacing of signal sampling period. Other parameters include: time t; the wavelet function $\Psi_{f.e}$ is used for frequency estimation; and $C(a_i, b_i)$ that are the wavelet coefficients with the specified scale and position parameters. Finally, the scale is converted to the mode frequency, f_m for each facial frame:

$$f_m = \frac{f_a\left(\Psi_{f.e}\right)}{a_m\left(\Psi_{f.e}\right).\Delta} \tag{7}$$

where $f_a\left(\Psi_{f.e}\right)$ is the average frequency of the wavelet function, and Δ is the signal sampling period. The feature vector is obtained by taking the average of the whole pixels distance for each facial frame that is given as:

$$f_{dist} = \frac{f_1 + f_2 + f_3 + ... + f_K}{N} \tag{8}$$

where f_{dist} indicates the average distance of each facial frame which is known as a feature vector of that expressions, f_1 f_2 f_3 .... f_K are the mode frequencies for each individual frame, K is the last frame of the current expression, and N represents the whole number of frames in each expression video.

In next step, the dimension of the feature space is reduced by employing a well-known technique Linear Discriminant Analysis (LDA) that maximizes the ratio of between-class variance to within-class variance in any particular data set, thereby guaranteeing maximal separability. For more details on LDA, please refer to [3].

2.2   Expression Modeling and Training Using HMM

HMM is a well-known method that provides a statistical model λ for a set of observation sequences. Sometimes, the observations are called "frames" in facial expression recognition applications. Suppose there are sequence of observations of length T that are denoted by $O_1, O_2, ..., O_T$. An HMM also consists of particular sequences of states, S, whose lengths range from 1 to N ($S = S_1, S_2, ..., S_N$), where N is the number of states in the model, and the time t for each state is denoted $Q = q_1, q_2, ..., q_N$. The likelihood $P\left(O|\lambda\right)$ can be evaluated by summing over all possible state sequences:

$$P\left(O|\lambda\right) = \sum_Q P(O, Q|\lambda) \tag{9}$$

A simple procedure for finding the parameters λ that maximize the above equation for HMMs, introduced in [2] depends on the forward and backward algorithms $\alpha_t(j) = P(O_1...O_t, q_t = j|\lambda)$ and $\beta_t(j) = P(O_(t+1)...O_T|q_t = j, \lambda)$, respectively, such that these variables can be initiated inductively by the following three processes:

$$\alpha_1(j) = \pi_j b_j(O_1), 1 \leq j \leq N \tag{10}$$

$$\beta_T(j) = 1, 1 \leq j \leq N \tag{11}$$

During testing, the appropriate HMMs can then be determined by mean of likelihood estimation for the sequence observations O calculated based on the trained λ as

$$P(O|\lambda) = \sum_{i=1}^{N} \alpha_T(i) \tag{12}$$

The maximum likelihood for the observations provided by the trained HMMs indicates the recognized label. For more details on HMM, please refer to [16].

3   Experimental Results and Discussion

We have tested the idea of employing symlet wavelet transform for human facial expression recognition in the study. The tests were found to be successful and we have achieved significant improvement in recognition rate. The proposed feature extraction has been tested and validated on publicly available standard dataset named Cohn-Kanade [8]. Six basic expressions were collected for experiments such as happy, anger, surprise, sad, disgust, and fear from this dataset that were performed by 40 different subjects. All these expressions in this dataset display the frontal view of the face. The size of each frame was 60x60, where the images were first converted to a zero-mean vector of size 1x3600 for feature extraction.

The system was trained and tested by employing n-fold cross validation rule based on subjects. It means that out of n subjects, data from a single subject was retained as the validation data for testing the proposed scheme, whereas the data for the remaining $n-1$ subjects were used as the training data. This process was repeated n times, with data from each subject used exactly once as the validation data. The value of n varied according to the dataset used. The total 2,880 ((6 x 40 x12), where 6 represents the number of expressions, 40 indicates the number of subjects, and 12 shows the frames in each expression video) frames are used for the whole experiments.

The performance of the proposed facial feature extraction technique has been validated by comparing it with some of the previous widely used well-known statistical techniques like: PCA, and ICA. The experimental results of the proposed technique along with results of the statistical methods are shown in Figure 1 and in Table 1 and 2.

It is obvious from Figure 1 and Table 1 that the proposed technique achieved best recognition rate than of the statistical methods as shown in Table 2.

Table 1. Confusion matrix of the proposed method on Cohn-Kanade database of facial expressions (Unit: %)

	Happy	Sad	Anger	Disgust	Surprise	Fear
Happy	94	3	0	0	1	2
Sad	2	95	0	3	0	0
Anger	0	3	93	0	0	4
Disgust	0	1	1	96	2	0
Surprise	0	2	0	3	92	4
Fear	0	0	4	2	0	94
Average			94			

Table 2. Confusion matrix of the statistical methods (like: PCA, ICA, LDA) with HMM using Cohn-Kanade database of facial expressions (Unit: %)

	Happy	Sad	Anger	Disgust	Surprise	Fear
Happy	86.1	6	2.5	3.4	2	0
Sad	5	89	0	3	0	3
Anger	0	0	91	3	0	6
Disgust	0	0	0	90.1	9.9	0
Surprise	2	0	0	6	88	4
Fear	2	1	15	2	0	80
Average			87.37			

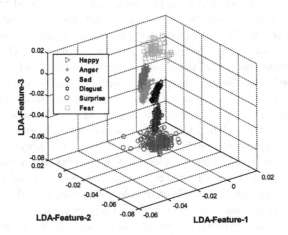

Fig. 1. 3D-feature plot for six different types of facial expressions after LDA. It is indicated that LDA provides best classification rate on the proposed feature extraction technique.

This is because symlet wavelet is a compactly supported wavelet on gray scale images with the least asymmetry and highest number of vanishing moments for a given support width. The symlet wavelet has the capability to support the characteristics of orthogonal, biorthogonal, and reverse biorthogonal of gray scale images, thats why it provides better classification results. The frequency-based assumption is supported in our experiments. We measure the statistic dependency of wavelet coefficients for all the facial frames of gray scale. Joint probability of a grey scale frame is computed by collecting geometrically aligned frames of the expression for each wavelet coefficient. Mutual information for the wavelet coefficients computed using these distributions is used to estimate the strength of statistical dependency between the two facial frames. Moreover, wavelet transform is capable to extract prominent features from gray scale images with the aid of locality in frequency, orientation and in space as well. Since wavelet is a multi-resolution that helps us to efficiently find the images in coarse-to-find way. Moreover, it is obvious from Figure 1 that applying LDA to features from all the classes provides best separation of the expressions. LDA is a linear technique, which limits its flexibility when applied to complex datasets. Moreover, LDA maximizes the total scatter of the data while minimizing the within scatter of the classes.

4   Conclusion

Facial Expressions Recognition (FER) has become an important research area for many applications over the last decade. A typical FER system consists of three basic modules such as preprocessing module that is used to improve the quality of the image by diminishing the illumination noise and by eliminating the unnecessary details from the background, feature extraction module that deals with getting the distinguishable features each expression and quantizing it as a discrete symbol, and recognition module, in which a classifier is first trained with training data and then used to generate the label of human facial expression contained in the incoming video data. Mostly, facial features are very sensitive to noise and illumination and quite merge with each other in the feature space, that's why in the feature space, it is very hard to separate the different facial expression features. Therefore, very less amount of work can be found be found on feature extraction module in literature. In this work, we proposed a new technique based on symlet wavelet for feature extraction module. In this technique, the human face is divided into number of regions and in each region the distance between the two pixels were calculated based on distance formula. After that, the average distance was found for each region and hence by this way the feature vectors were created. To reduce the dimensions of the feature vectors in the feature space, LDA was exploited. Finally, the expressions were labeled by employing HMM. The proposed system achieved an average recognition accuracy of 94% over Cohn-Kanade dataset, illustrating the successful employment of the proposed method for FER system. In the proposed technique, n-fold cross validation rule has been exploited to achieve best accuracy. The proposed FER system has been trained and tested in laboratory. The next step will be the implementation of the proposed feature extraction technique in smarthomes or in smartphones for real healthcare environment.

References

1. Bartlett, M.S., Donato, G., Movellan, J.R., Hager, J.C., Ekman, P., Sejnowski, T.J.: Face image analysis for expression measurement and detection of deceit. In: Proceedings of the 6th Annual Joint Symposium on Neural Computation (1999)
2. Baum, L.E.: An equality and associated maximization technique in statistical estimation for probabilistic functions of markov processes. Inequalities 3, 1–8 (1972)
3. Belhumeur, P.N., Hespanha, J.P., Kriegman, D.J.: Eigenfaces vs. fisherfaces: Recognition using class specific linear projection. IEEE Transactions on Pattern Analysis and Machine Intelligence 19(7), 711–720 (1997)
4. Chuang, C.-F., Shih, F.Y.: Recognizing facial action units using independent component analysis and support vector machine. Pattern Recognition 39(9), 1795–1798 (2006)
5. Donato, G., Bartlett, M.S., Hager, J.C., Ekman, P., Sejnowski, T.J.: Classifying facial actions. IEEE Transactions on Pattern Analysis and Machine Intelligence 21(10), 974–989 (1999)
6. Fasel, B., Luettin, J.: Automatic facial expression analysis: a survey. Pattern Recognition 36(1), 259–275 (2003)
7. Feng, G.C., Yuen, P.C., Dai, D.Q.: Human face recognition using pca on wavelet subband. Journal of Electronic Imaging 9(2), 226–233 (2000)
8. Kanade, T., Cohn, J.F., Tian, Y.: Comprehensive database for facial expression analysis. In: Proceedings of the Fourth IEEE International Conference on Automatic Face and Gesture Recognition, pp. 46–53. IEEE (2000)
9. Kaur, M., Vashisht, R.: Comparative study of facial expression recognition techniques. International Journal of Computer Applications 13(1) (2011)
10. Kim, J., Choi, J., Yi, J., Turk, M.: Effective representation using ica for face recognition robust to local distortion and partial occlusion. IEEE Transactions on Pattern Analysis and Machine Intelligence 27(12), 1977–1981 (2005)
11. Li, S.Z., Hou, X.W., Zhang, H.J., Cheng, Q.S.: Learning spatially localized, parts-based representation. In: Proceedings of the 2001 IEEE Computer Society Conference on Computer Vision and Pattern Recognition, CVPR 2001, vol. 1, p. I-207. IEEE (2001)
12. Lin, D.-T.: Facial expression classification using pca and hierarchical radial basis function network. Journal of Information Science and Engineering 22(5), 1033–1046 (2006)
13. Lin, D.-T.: Human facial expression recognition using hybrid network of PCA and RBFN. In: Kollias, S.D., Stafylopatis, A., Duch, W., Oja, E. (eds.) ICANN 2006. LNCS, vol. 4132, pp. 624–633. Springer, Heidelberg (2006)
14. Mehrabian, A.: Communication without words. Psychological Today 2, 53–55 (1968)
15. Penev, P.S., Atick, J.J.: Local feature analysis: A general statistical theory for object representation. Network: Computation in Neural Systems 7(3), 477–500 (1996)
16. Samaria, F.S.: Face recognition using hidden Markov models. PhD thesis, University of Cambridge (1994)
17. Turunen, J., et al.: A wavelet-based method for estimating damping in power systems (2011)

A Real-Time Insulin Injection System

Mwaffaq Otoom[1], Hussam Alshraideh[2], Hisham M. Almasaeid[1],
Diego López-de-Ipiña[3], and José Bravo[4]

[1] Yarmouk University, Jordan
[2] Jordan University of Science and Technology, Jordan
[3] University of Deusto, Spain
[4] Castilla-La Mancha University, Spain

Abstract. We develop a prototype for real-time blood sugar control based upon the hypothesis that there is a medical challenge in determining the exact, real-time insulin dose. Our system controls blood sugar by observing the blood sugar level and automatically determining the appropriate insulin dose based on patient's historical data all in real time. At the heart of our system is an algorithm that determines the appropriate insulin dose. Our algorithm consists of two phases. In the first phase, the algorithm identifies the insulin dose offline using a Markov Process based model. In the other phase, it recursively trains the web hosted Markov model to adapt to different human bodies' responsiveness.

Keywords: Diabetes, Insulin Management, Markov Processes, Web Management.

1 Introduction

Three hundred forty seven million people worldwide have diabetes [15]. The World Health Organization predicts that diabetes will be the seventh leading cause of death in 2030. Furthermore, during their lifetime, diabetics may suffer from a devastating damage to many of their body systems, leading to hardships not just for the diabetics themselves but also for their families and national economies. Such damages include, but not limited to, cardiovascular, foot ulcers, diabetic retinopathy, and kidney failure [7].

Blood sugar level for an individual is a function of multiple factors including demographics, diet, exercises, and medications. Medically, determining the proper insulin dose is done in an ad-hoc manner by a diabetes consultant [9]. Since most of the aforementioned factors are varying over time, the determination of insulin dose becomes a continuous process that needs medical supervision and intervention, on almost a daily basis. It is worth pointing out that the responsiveness to the same dose of insulin may vary among patients, even if they share the same conditions mentioned earlier.

One key solution to stop the negative effects of diabetes is the continuous administration of insulin. However, it is usually difficult for elderly, inexperienced

C. Nugent, A. Coronato, and J. Bravo (Eds.): IWAAL 2013, LNCS 8277, pp. 120–127, 2013.

people to maintain this continuity on a daily basis. Furthermore, there is a medical challenge to determine the exact, real-time insulin dose required to compensate the deficiency of insulin production or inefficiency of insulin absorption [17].

To handle these challenges, in this paper we develop, for insulin-dependent diabetics, a prototype for real-time blood sugar control. At real time, our system controls blood sugar by observing the blood sugar level and automatically determining the appropriate insulin dose based on patient's historical data. Our system consists mainly of two parts: a web server and a client. The web component is responsible for the recursive training of the blood sugar model, while the client is responsible for sugar monitoring and insulin injection in addition to communication with the web server. At the heart of our proposed system is the algorithm that determines the appropriate insulin dose for a specific blood sugar level, which is considered the most challenging step in diabetes medication.

The rest of the paper is organized as follows. A review of relevant literature is given in section 2. In section 3 we develop a Markov Process based model for blood sugar data. Section 4 presents the architecture of the proposed blood sugar control system. Finally, conclusions and future recommendations are given in section 5.

2 Literature Review

Modeling medical data has become a cornerstone in various advancements in the medical field including medicine development, patient monitoring, disease tracking and avoidance, and many others [12]. Most of the existing models are statistical and based on a pool of historical data collected from the related parties. Under some circumstances, data collection may have to be a real-time process. That applies, for example, to situations where there is a need to predict the change in some medical measures (blood pressure, glucose level, etc) to predict and consequently proactively deal with life-threatening conditions that patients may face.

The rapid technological advancements made in the past few years have paved the way for a significant volume of initiatives and proposals to integrate the health and ICT (Information and Communication Technologies) sectors into what is referred to nowadays as the *eHealth* world [16], [2]. This integration is expected to make, and in fact has already made, significant improvements in health care. This improvement is attributed not only to the quality of the provided care, but also to its effect on the economy [1].

Diabetes has spread widely across the world in the past few decades, which motivated the research community to benefit from the aforementioned integration between ICT and Health care to come up with new solutions for diabetics [8], [12]. In this paper, we study the problem of determining the insulin dose for diabetic patients. A number of proposals which tackled the same problem have appeared in literature over the past few years [4], [3], [11]. In [3], the authors propose a neural network model of a set of rules devised by health specialists to determine the insulin dose. The model relies on short sets of historical data to train the neural network. The difference between our proposal and the proposals in [4], [3], [11] is twofold. First, we use an online estimation algorithm based on a Markov model that continuously updates itself with the observed historical data. Second, we incorporated the use of modern technology to facilitate the use of the system for patients. In our system, the collected historical data is automatically transferred to an online server for processing without external intervention (beyond initial setup). The estimated next dose is also calculated automatically by a mobile application installed on a patient's smart phone, and the pump is activated without user intervention.

3   Markov Processes for Modeling Blood Sugar Level

In statistics, the collection of a random variable X over an index set T is called a stochastic process [10]. For example, the collection of weather temperature observations over a period of time is a stochastic process. In most applications, T is the time spots at which the random variable of interest is being observed. If the index set T consists of discrete values and the values that the random variable X can have is also discrete, then the stochastic process is called a discrete time discrete space stochastic process.

A stochastic process that satisfies the Markovian property, that is:

$$P(X_{t+1} = j \mid X_0 = x_0, X_1 = x_1, \cdots, X_t = i) = \qquad (1)$$
$$P(X_{t+1} = j \mid X_t = i)$$

is called a Markov Process. This property implies that the future value of the random variable depends on its history only through the current observation [13]. The values that X can have are called the states. The right hand side of (1) reads as the probability that the process will move to state j given that the process is currently at state i. This probability is usually abbreviated as p_{ij} and is called the transition probability. For a Markov process with n possible states, the transition probabilities p_{ij} can be concatenated in a matrix form called the transition matrix [10] such that:

$$P = \begin{pmatrix} p_{11} & p_{12} & \cdots & p_{1n} \\ p_{21} & p_{22} & \cdots & p_{2n} \\ \vdots & \vdots & \vdots & \vdots \\ p_{n1} & p_{n2} & \cdots & p_{nn} \end{pmatrix} \qquad (2)$$

The transition probability p_{ij} is estimated using the Frequentist approach as the ratio of the number of transitions from state i to state j to the total number of transitions from state i.

Let the random variable SL represent the blood sugar level and assume that SL is observed at several time spots. The set of observations of SL form a stochastic process. Furthermore, assume that the next value of SL depends on previous history through its current value, then this is a Markov Process. Normal

Table 1. Experimental setup for the amount of carbohydrates intake factors for the three daily meals

Day	Breakfast	Lunch	Dinner	Day	Breakfast	Lunch	Dinner
1	30	60	30	15	60	120	90
2	30	60	60	16	60	180	30
3	30	60	90	17	60	180	60
4	30	120	30	18	60	180	90
5	30	120	60	19	90	60	30
6	30	120	90	20	90	60	60
7	30	180	30	21	90	60	90
8	30	180	60	22	90	120	30
9	30	180	90	23	90	120	60
10	60	60	30	24	90	120	90
11	60	60	60	25	90	180	30
12	60	60	90	26	90	180	60
13	60	120	30	27	90	180	90
14	60	120	60				

blood sugar level ranges from 80 to 120 mg/dl. For diabetics, blood sugar level could go down as low as 20 mg/dl or up as high as 500 mg/dl and more. For a modeling purpose, we assume a range of 0 to 600 for blood sugar level. The assumed range is discretized into 121 states of values $\{0, 5, 10, 15, \cdots, 595, 600\}$.

An experiment for blood sugar profiles generation was conducted at one of the Jordanian hospitals. The experiment consisted of four factors. These were the body weight, the amount of carbohydrates intake at breakfast, the amount of carbohydrates intake at lunch and the amount of carbohydrates intake at dinner. Three levels for the body weight factor were considered, 100 lb, 200 lb and 300 lb. One patient of each body weight category was volunteered for the study. The amount of carbohydrates intake at breakfast and dinner was changed at three levels of 30, 60 and 90 grams, while the amount of carbohydrates intake at lunch was changed at three levels of 60, 120 and 180 grams. Assuming a factorial design, each of the three patients was under study for 27 days. For each day the amount of carbohydrates intake for the three daily meals was changed according to the experimental setup shown in Table 1 and the blood sugar level was observed every half an hour for the 24 hours period of the day resulting in 81 sugar profiles. These sugar profiles were used to estimate the transition probabilities for the Markov Process assumed.

For validation, the built Markov chain model was used to estimate several blood sugar profiles. The estimated versus the actual data of two sugar profiles are shown in Figure 1. These plots show that the model is capable of providing acceptable blood sugar estimates.

The estimated transition matrix will be stored on the smart mobile device which will be connected to the sugar sensor wirelessly. At a given time spot, the sensor measures the current blood sugar level and send it to the mobile device. The implemented algorithm on the mobile device estimates the next sugar level

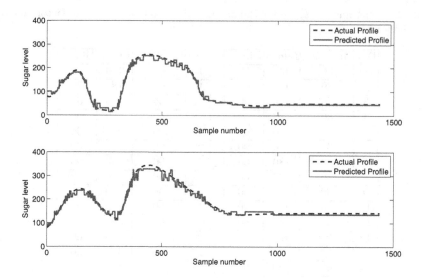

Fig. 1. Actual versus estimated sugar profiles used for model validation

reading (the reading at the next time spot) based on the current blood sugar reading. Estimating the next sugar reading is done through two steps. In the first step the current sugar level reading is assigned to one of the 121 states mentioned above. At the second step, given the current state from the first step and the transition matrix one can estimate the next sugar level as the expected value of the next state. That is the sum over the probable next states of the next state sugar level multiplied by the probability to move to it. Knowing the probable next sugar level reading, insulin dose is determined accordingly taking into account previous insulin injections.

The readings from the sugar sensor are stored on the mobile device. Once every n-days, the stored readings are transmitted to the web server where the transition matrix is updated on a patient-aware manner then the updated transition matrix is sent back to the mobile device.

4   System Architecture

Our overall goal is to precisely determine the required insulin dose for a specific patient, taking into consideration that different diabetics respond to insulin differently. Existing approaches rely mainly on specialist consultation [6]. Other automated approaches consider only giving notifications on oncoming highs and lows without real time insulin dose determination and injection [6]. Up to our knowledge, none of existing approaches has considered sharing patients sugar history online for tracking and monitoring.

Our solution to achieve this goal is by using a web based framework that enables the patient's data to be communicated via web with specialists, research

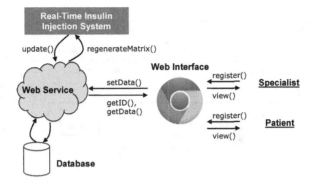

Fig. 2. System Overview

institutes, and more significantly with an automated system that computes the required insulin dose based on the sugar levels history of the patient.

Figure 2 shows an overview of our system in which the Real-Time Insulin Injection System (RTIIS) communicates the patient's data with the server via a web service. The RTIIS updates the database via the **update()** web method with patient's sugar levels periodically with period T_u which can be configured at RTIIS. Upon receiving new updates, the server runs our suggested algorithm that is based on Markov Chains, to regenerate the transition matrix that we use in the RTIIS to identify the required insulin dose. The RTIIS can then fetch the updated matrix by calling the **regenerateMatrix()**, web method at the server. Again, this call is made every period T_u. Note that all data is stored in the database and can be viewed via a web dashboard by both the specialist and the patient. To do so, we build a web interface that can be used to register a patient or a specialist and to view data. Once registered, specialist and patient will receive an ID that can be used to access the web interface. The patient ID is also used to establish the connection between the RTIIS and the web service.

Figure 3 depicts our suggested system and illustrates its functionality step by step. Our system consists of three hardware components: glucose sensor, mobile phone, and pump, all are Bluetooth enabled. The glucose sensor continuously sends sugar readings, SL(t), via Bluetooth. The mobile phone which hosts the injection application receives SL readings via Bluetooth, as well. The mobile application saves each reading in history and processes it. Processing sugar level readings is simple. Using the estimated transition matrix, for a given sugar reading the application predicts the next reading using the expected value method. We define the required insulin dose, IU, as the insulin units required to dispose the difference sugar between the expected value and the current value. Once the IU is identified, the mobile application sends this value to the pump that is connected to the patient's body. The pump, in turn, pumps IU units of insulin into patient's body. As described in Figure 2, the mobile application also sends the stored sugar history to a server via a web service. We choose to update the

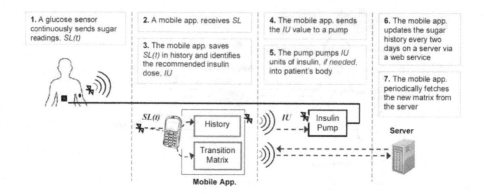

Fig. 3. The Real Time Insulin Injection System

history on server every two days to make sure that the given insulin is precise as well as to clear the history from the limited size memory of the cell phone. Finally, the mobile application gets the updated transition matrix.

5   Conclusion

Diabetes is one of the fastest growing diseases since many endeavors, so far, have not been successful to not just find a solution but also to manage the devastating effects caused by this disease on human health. The other trend we are facing today is the tremendous change in technology and its engagement in human health systems. The intersection of these two trends has inspired us to come up with a novel approach that contributes to Diabetes negative effects management.

Our approach integrates mobile phone, web, and sensor technologies to help a diabetic to automatically administer insulin injection; something is considered a burden in Diabetes medication. While our approach is effective, it is simple. Simplicity comes from two features: (1) the utilization of the ubiquity of mobile, sensor, and Internet technologies, (2) the algorithm we developed to control the blood sugar level is computationally inexpensive.

For future work we intend to evaluate the performance of other time series modeling algorithms. Further, we plan to measure the quality of life for patients using our system through the Diabetics Quality of Life Questionnaire (DQLQ).

References

1. Akematsu, Y., Tsuji, M.: Economic effect of eHealth: Focusing on the reduction of days spent for treatment. In: 11th International Conference on e-Health Networking, Applications and Services, Healthcom 2009 (2009)
2. Alasaarela, E., Nemana, R., DeMello, S.: Drivers and challenges of wireless solutions in future healthcare. In: International Conference on eHealth, Telemedicine, and Social Medicine

3. Andrianasy, F., Milgram, M.: Applying neural networks to adjust insulin-pump doses. In: Proceedings of the 1997 IEEE Workshop Neural Networks for Signal Processing VII (1997)
4. Campos-Cornejo, F., Campos-Delgado, D.U.: Self-Tuning Insulin Dosing Algorithm for Glucose Regulation in Type 1 Diabetic Patients. In: Pan American Health Care Exchanges, PAHCE 2009 (2009)
5. Jordanova, M.M.: eHealth: from space medicine to civil healthcare. In: Proceedings of 2nd International Conference on Recent Advances in Space Technologies, RAST 2005 (2005)
6. King, A.B., Clark, D., Wolfe, G.S.: How much do I give? Dose estimation formulas for once-nightly insulin glargine and premeal insulin lispro in type 1 diabetes mellitus. Endocrine Practice 18(3), 382–386 (2012)
7. Klonoff, D.C., Buse, J.B., Nielsen, L.L., Guan, X., Bowlus, C.L., Holcombe, J.H., Maggs, D.G.: Exenatide effects on diabetes, obesity, cardiovascular risk factors and hepatic biomarkers in patients with type 2 diabetes treated for at least 3 years. Current Medical Research and Opinion 24(1), 275–286 (2007)
8. Wang, N., Kang, G.: A monitoring system for type 2 diabetes mellitus. In: IEEE 14th International Conference on e-Health Networking, Applications and Service (Healthcom)
9. Rizza, R.A., Mandarino, L.J., Gerich, J.E.: Dose-response characteristics for effects of insulin on production and utilization of glucose in man. American Journal of Physiology-Endocrinology and Metabolism 240(6), E630–E639 (1981)
10. Ross, S.M.: Introduction to Probability Models, 10th edn. Elsevier AP (2010)
11. Shimauchi, T., Kugai, N., Nagata, N., Takatani, O.: Microcomputer-aided insulin dose determination in intensified conventional insulin therapy. IEEE Transactions on Biomedical Engineering (2013)
12. Stein, O.S., Eirik, A., Ragnar, M.J., Fred, G.: Statistical Modeling of Aggregated Lifestyle and Blood Glucose Data in Type 1 Diabetes Patients. In: Second International Conference on eHealth, Telemedicine, and Social Medicine (2010)
13. Taha, H.A.: Operations Research: An Introduction, 9th edn. Prentice Hall, New Jersey (2010)
14. Pickup, J.C.: Insulin-pump therapy for type 1 diabetes mellitus. New England Journal of Medicine 366(17), 1616–1624 (2012)
15. http://who.int/mediacentre/factsheets/fs312/en/index.html (accessed on July 2013)
16. Vasilyeva, E., Pechenizkiy, M., Puuronen, S.: Towards the framework of adaptive user interfaces for eHealth. In: Proceedings of 18th IEEE Symposium on Computer-Based Medical Systems (2005)
17. Wallace, T.M., Matthews, D.R.: The assessment of insulin resistance in man. Diabetic Medicine 19(7), 527–534 (2002)

Development and Evaluation of an Augmented Object for Notifications of Particular Emails

Gustavo López Herrera, Mariana López, and Luis A. Guerrero

Centro de Investigaciones en Tecnologías de la Información y Comunicación, UCR
Escuela de Ciencias de la Computación e Informática, UCR
gustavo.lopez_h@ucr.ac.cr,
{mariana.lopez,luis.guerrero}@ecci.ucr.ac.cr

Abstract. Email is an essential tool for most of the people. However, the amount of messages, including spam, we receive every day complicates our ability to concentrate on messages we consider important. In this project we design and develop a prototype of an augmented object that notifies users when important mail arrives. The process of design, development and testing is described and discussed in this paper.

Keywords: Ambient Intelligence, Augmented Objects, Ubiquitous Computing.

1 Introduction

Many examples of augmented objects have been developed in the last years focusing on different areas like health [3], education [2] and daily activities [1]. These objects are becoming more common in our lives and more people are using them. However one of the key issues in this area is how to design and construct "well" augmented objects, that is, augmented objects that solve the specific problem and that can be used in an easily and intuitive manner. In this way, Guerrero et al. [4] proposed a process for designing and developing augmented objects.

In this research project we were faced with the problem of creating an augmented object to help notify if important emails arrive. This paper presents our experiences in the process of building this augmented object prototype. The next section presents how the prototype was designed and developed. Section 3 shows our testing method. Conclusions are presented in section 4.

2 Design and Development of the Augmented Object

The networked electronic mail (email) has been developing for the past 40 years and many perspectives have been taken into consideration for the development of the email but most of the effort has been made in the technical aspects and not the usability of the email [6]. In the past few years mail companies have made changes in the user interfaces of the mail service but as far as we know no physical displays of mail have been made.

C. Nugent, A. Coronato, and J. Bravo (Eds.): IWAAL 2013, LNCS 8277, pp. 128–131, 2013.
© Springer International Publishing Switzerland 2013

Since users have developed a dependency on electronic communications and there are many companies providing email services we found a necessity of easy access to the mail information and most importantly a distinction between spam, normal mail and "important" mails. To address this problem, we will define "important mails" as mails received from an "important person". The user can define these "important persons". In future work it would be important to dive into better and more complex filters that can be added to the prototype, but for the purpose of this paper and experiment we focused only on the notification method.

For the first version of the prototype we decided that the context of use of the final system should be the work office or the user's house. That is, the object will be designed for and tested in these two places. The three main requirements were: (1) The system must be able to determine if any of the arriving mails were sent by an important person and the user should be notified; (2) The system should display part of the text of the mail in order to allow the user to know if it is really important or urgent. Some of the displayed information can be: sender, issue, first lines, attachments, hour, etc. (3) The user must be able to configure simple system settings, for instance: maximum quantity of notifications and definition of important senders.

With the requirements and the context of use defined, the process of selecting the augmented object started. Following the Augmented Object Development Process (AODeP) [4] we use a model for a syntactic and semantic analysis on every object in the context of use in order to determine which one will be the best candidate to be augmented. Some of the possible candidates were: key holder, clipboard, penholder, post-its notes. Using the syntactic and semantic charts proposed in AODeP we discovered that the best object to use were the post-it notes. This selection was due to the metaphor of a real notification. Post-it notes are a general accepted method for giving notifications, for instance, in the refrigerator, in a board, or even in the computer monitor. According to this, we decided that the best candidate would be a physical post-it note in the user's monitor.

The implemented configuration system consists of three different screens. The first one validates the user login and password. The second one is a configuration panel that allows the user to modify the list of important contacts either add an important contact or delete it from the important list. Finally a third screen allows the user to see how many important mails he/she has, who the senders are, and what the issue is. Figure 1 shows the configuration screen of the system.

Once the system was implemented the development of the object began. We use Phidgets to build a prototype (a servo and a controller). Figure 2 shows the augmented post-it. This object needs to be hooked to the back part of the monitor so that, when the servo moves the cable, the post-it note appears over the monitor (see right picture in figure 2). Otherwise it is not visible from the front of the screen.

It is important to note that the system that controls the post-it is not 100% autonomous and movable in this prototype, and the user must run a daemon on the computer in order for the post-it to work. A further version of the prototype could consider a Wi-Fi connection to give more autonomy to the object (for instance, for working even if the computer is turned off). Right picture in Figure 2 shows how the post-it note looks like when an important message arrives to the inbox. The note said (in Spanish): "You have mail in Gmail".

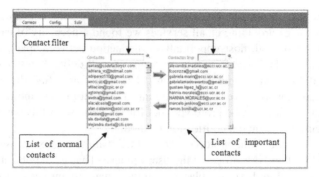

Fig. 1. Web system: Configuration Screen

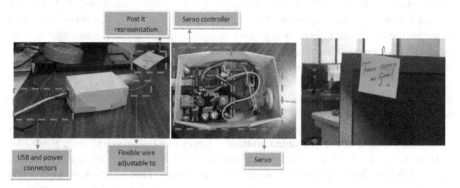

Fig. 2. Hardware of the augmented post-it

When the user checks his/her mail and open the message, the servo moves the post-it back to the monitor. Using this trick, we create the sensation that a post-it note appears and disappears from the monitor of the user.

3   Validating the Augmented Object

Once the augmented post-it was developed we wanted to validate if this object would be useful for our users. An augmented post-it was located in the work desk for a user that wasn't part of the development team. We monitored the system's performance for 5 days, 8 hours a day. As a result, we found that: (1) The prototype stops working when Windows enters hibernation mode; (2) If the user closes the session the daemon that controls the post-it stops working; (3) If the machine is turned off the prototype stops working.

Although, the user liked the prototype we had to fix these technical errors to test further. We changed some settings in the application so that the process didn't stop even when hibernation mode was on and so that it ran automatically when the computer was turned on. After the functional test we designed a second testing phase using four prototypes. We gave the four prototypes to four administrative personnel.

Due to the nature of the task at hand, we decided the best approach was to conduct a test that would allow our participants to record their experience with the prototype. Therefore we decided the best approach to evaluate the prototypes was to conduct a Diary Study. We asked selected participants to keep a diary of the prototype usage over the course of 8 days, the objective was to test the prototype in context at different stages of our users day and throughout several days. The diary contains sets of 5 questions that the user would answer each time an important email was received. The questions asked if the user was using the computer in the moment that s/he received the email, what was s/he doing, or if s/he was away where was s/he. Other questions were the mail delivery hour and the hour s/he saw the notification and the last one was if the mail was really important.

The feedback we received about the augmented object was positive; all the users found the system very useful and asked for Wi-Fi versions of the next prototype.

4   Conclusions and Further Work

We can conclude the augmented post-it prototype solved the initial requirements. The testing of the actual prototype is not always straightforward and that if it is to be tested in actual user context, certain techniques, like diary studies, must be implemented so that the task is not artificial and the results are measurable. As a further work, the prototype will be improved based on users feedback. We need also to work on the usability of the augmented objects and the communication interface to set up variables for retrieving specific email.

Acknowledgments. This work was supported by grant No. 834-B2-228 from CITIC-UCR (Costa Rica).

References

1. Alamán, X., Ballesteros, F., Bravo, J., Fernández, D.: Ambient Intelligence at Home: Facts and Future. Cepis Upgrade: Ambient Intelligence. Novatica 8(4), 13–18 (2007)
2. Ananny, M., Cassell, J.: Telling Tales: A new toy for encouraging written literacy through oral storytelling. Society for Research in Child Development, Minnesota (April 2001)
3. Gasca, E., Favela, J., Tentori, M.: Assisting Support Groups of Patients with Chronic Diseases through Persuasive Computing. J. of Universal Computer Science 15(16) (2009)
4. Guerrero, L., Ochoa, S., Horta, H.: Developing Augmented Objects: A Process Perspective. Journal of Universal Computer Science 16(12), 1612–1632 (2010)
5. Partridge, C.: The Technical Development of Internet Email. IEEE Annals of the History of Computing 30(2), 3–29 (2008)

An Augmented Object Prototype for Helping to Prevent the Sudden Infant Death Syndrome

Gustavo López, Mariana López, and Luis A. Guerrero

Centro de Investigaciones en Tecnologías de la Información y Comunicación, UCR
Escuela de Ciencias de la Computación e Informática, UCR
gustavo.lopez_h@ucr.ac.cr,
{mariana.lopez,luis.guerrero}@ecci.ucr.ac.cr

Abstract. The Sudden Infant Death Syndrome causes unexpected death of infants. Some of the risk factors are related to the prone or side sleeping, ambient temperature and bedclothes overhead, among others. We state that some of these risk factors can be sensed using an augmented object in the bedclothes of the infants, and that the collected information can be sent to an adult through a mobile application. In this paper we present a prototype with sensor-base interfaces that can prevent the Sudden Infant Death Syndrome.

Keywords: Sensor-based interfaces, Augmented Objects, Ubiquitous Computing, Healthcare.

1 Introduction

Sudden Infant Death Syndrome (SIDS) is the unexpected death of infants from birth to first year of age. Usually, the syndrome causes death and pathologies cannot be determined, even after thorough investigation. Not long ago 1 or 2 kids per every 1000 lost their lives because SIDS. However, there has been an active group of people working to make the SIDS lethality drop but nowadays the syndrome still causes death in up to 0.8 children every 1000 births [1].

The Institute for Clinical Systems Improvement (www.icsi.org) created a health care guideline for children and adolescents. In the 2012 edition of that document they explain that infant sleep position is very important for decreasing SIDS risks. A key takeaway of their investigation is that parents should put the infants to bed in a back sleeping position, because stomach or side sleeping can increase the risk of SIDS occurring [2].

An interesting fact is that many SIDS affected children die when they are with their nanny. This may be due to the fact that the nanny places the baby in the stomach sleeping position and the baby is not accustomed to being placed in that position [1]. According to Tintinalli et al. [1], some of the main risk factors for SIDS are the following: Prone or side sleeping, bedclothes over head, sleeping on sofa or soft furniture, high or low ambient temperature, soft bedding, bed sharing, postnatal smoke exposure, prenatal smoke, alcohol, or drug exposure.

C. Nugent, A. Coronato, and J. Bravo (Eds.): IWAAL 2013, LNCS 8277, pp. 132–135, 2013.

We state that some of the risk factors mentioned above can be sensed using a special object with several sensors, like temperature sensors and accelerometers, and the collected information can be sent through a mobile application to the father, mother or someone else. This paper focuses on the design, implementation and evaluation of an augmented object prototype combined with a mobile application that help prevent some of the risk factors associated with the SIDS syndrome.

The next section will show the augmented object design, as well as the components and systems architecture. Section 3 presents the evaluation of the prototype and section 4 presents our conclusions.

2   Developing the Augmented Object Prototype

As it was mentioned before, two of the main risk factors for SIDS are prone or side sleeping and high or low ambient temperature. Regarding those factors we want to provide an augmented object that monitors the position of the baby and the environments temperature in order to ensure the baby's safety.

Given that problem, the next step was to determine and analyze the possible use context, that is, the environmental characteristics of the places the object will be used in, for instance, the baby's room in the house, or the hospital room.

The object would start measuring when it is turned on by the responsible person and would notify if the sensed parameters indicate a potential risk: the baby is face down, high or low temperature. After studying the usage context the third step is the requirement definition, for this particular case study we determined the requirements were: (1) The alerts should be associated with one baby; (2) The responsible adult must be able to check position information about the baby; (3) The responsible adult must be able to check temperature data of the baby's environment, and (4) The responsible adult must be able to receive the information and alerts.

The next step in the process was the identification of the candidate objects to augment. Some of the candidates we identified were: a blanket, a clasp-pin, a pajama, a white tank, the crib, a clothing patch or a belt. Regarding the notifications, three possible objects were defined: a baby monitor, a mobile phone, and an alarm clock.

After discussing the possible objects we defined that the best object to augment was a clothing patch with Velcro and a mobile phone. The patch can be stuck to the baby pajama, and a mobile application can receive the notifications.

2.1   Designing the Augmented Object and Components

Once we selected the best candidate object to augment and the desirable new characteristics, we built a prototype. Figure 1 shows the components we used in the development of the augmented object prototype.

We set all the parts inside a bear cloth patch and left the cable for power and USB connection, a led was used to notify that the object is on; a button on the bear's hand is used to turn the bear patch on or off.

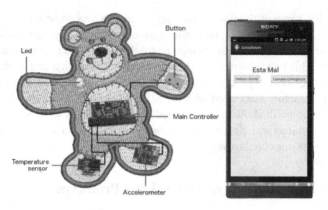

Fig. 1. Augmented object scheme and mobile interface

2.2   App Interface

As we mentioned above the parent's phone uses an application to receive the baby's data 24/7. Sensors on the baby capture the data, and it is shown to the user. The application allows the user to see the baby's state at all times, if anything is wrong the parent's phone will immediately start to ring and the application will appear in the foreground of the phone. There are two buttons on the application (see figure 1): the left one is "Stop Alert" and is used to stop the sound of the alarm. The right button is for an "Emergency call" that will immediately call the house were the baby is at. This number can be configured. The message *"Esta mal"* (in Spanish) means that the baby might be in trouble (in a potentially risk position).

3   Evaluating the Augmented Object Prototype

Before building the physical prototype of the augmented object we decided to validate the concept. In this process some interrogations emerged like: Which is the safest position for a baby? Which exact tilt degree is dangerous? Is the phone app important or are notifications only necessary near the baby's location? What is the correct size for the object given that it will be adhered to a baby? Where is the correct place to put the patch in the body? What would happen if the baby moves a lot?

In order to answer these questions we decided to use a Wizard of Oz validation [3]. Wizard of Oz is a technique for validating new ideas and evaluating prototypes. A simulation in which participants are given the impression that they are interacting with an actual system, however, participants are actually interacting with humans, which pretend to be the system.

We designed a Wizard of Oz study with our prototype. A group of people performed the role of wizard and simulated different situations with the baby at random hours. Our Wizards were given the task to tilt the dolls position at random times and our participants were tasked with keeping their baby alive, calling to check if they noticed that something was wrong in the babies' environment.

Each session consisted of a timeframe where the caregiver was away from the baby and had to monitor the environment remotely with the mobile device. In the post session interviews we verified if the information appeared to be timely and enough.

We also tested the prototype on a real baby, who was monitored at all times. The purpose of this experiment was to determinate the best position for the augmented object and to evaluate if it was comfortable for the baby. We conclude the baby is not able to take the object off or turn it off, and that they are able to sleep comfortably.

This prototype was a proof of concept, and even this early version worked fine at notifying the baby's state. One of the goals in the design of the application was that the interfaces were usable and straightforward. In this version the message has only two possibilities: the baby is in a normal position or in a risky one. The alarm is triggered when the sensor detects the baby tilts 90 degrees.

We found this sensor-based interface could be unobtrusive and very useful at gathering the required information, users felt comfortable with the information provided.

4   Conclusions and Further Work

In this paper we have presented the development of an augmented object prototype that can successfully notify caregivers of changes in the baby's environment. This prototype focuses mainly on sensor-based interfaces due to the requirements of the case study and is successful in monitoring the environment. We consider that the sensor-based interface for the developed app works fine.

Future work for this project could include incorporating the feedback received during the Wizard of Oz study to improve the accuracy and confidence level of the device in the eyes of the baby's primary caregivers.   As well as refining the prototype to be a standalone application that could be attached to any piece of baby clothing.

Acknowledgment. This work was supported by grand No. 834-B2-228 from CITIC-UCR (Costa Rica).

References

1. Tintinalli, J.E., Stapczynski, J.S., Cline, D.M., Ma, O.J., Cydulka, R.K., Meckler, G.D.: Tintinalli's Emergency Medicine: A Comprehensive Study Guide. In: The American College of Emergency Physicians, 7th edn. (2011)
2. Wilkinson, J., Bass, C., Diem, S., Gravley, A., Harvey, L., Hayes, R., Johnson, K., Maciosek, M., McKeon, K., Milteer, L., Morgan, J., Rothe, P., Snellman, L., Solberg, L., Storlie, C., Vincent, P.: Preventive Services for Children and Adolescents. Institute for Clinical Systems Improvement (2012)
3. Kelley, J.F.: An iterative design methodology for user-friendly natural language office information applications. ACM Transactions on Information Systems 2(1), 26–41 (1984)

Author Index